Target English

Reading

Developing Reader and Competent Reader

Teacher Guide

Helen Lines and Bekah Mardall

Heinemann

Heinemann is an imprint of Harcourt Education Limited, a company incorporated in England and Wales, having its registered office: Halley Court, Jordan Hill, Oxford OX2 8EJ. Registered company number: 3099304

www.harcourt.co.uk

Heinemann is the registered trademark of Harcourt Education Limited

First published 2007

12 11 10 09 08 07
10 9 8 7 6 5 4 3 2

British Library Cataloguing in Publication Data is available from the British Library on request.

ISBN 978 0435118 62 4

Minimum System Requirements
PC

- Processor: 900mhz Intel Pentium III, (Vista 1GHz Pentium 4 or equivalent)
- OS: Windows 2000 Professional, Windows XP Professional, Windows Vista
- Memory: 256MB, (Vista Home Basic 512 MB, other Vista versions 1GB)
- Screen Resolution: 800x600
- Microsoft Word 1997 or above.

For further software support between the hours of 8.30 - 5.30 (Mon - Fri) please contact:

- Tel: 01865-888108
- Fax: 01865-314091
- Email: software.enquiries@harcourt.co.uk

Layout by TAG Publishing Services

Original illustrations © Harcourt Education
Illustrated by Kathy Baxendale, Chris Brown, Paco Cavero, Janos Jantner, Gillian Martin, Sam Thompson, Mark Turner and Rory Walker

Cover design by Zannah Hawdon

Cover photo/illustration © Photdisc / Superstock
Printed in the UK by Ashford Colour Press

Acknowledgements
The authors and publisher would like to thank the following individuals and organisations for permission to reproduce photographs:

Getty Images / Matthias Clamer / Stone p25; NASA p38; Ralph A. Clevenger / CORBIS p47; PhotoDisc. Photolink p49; Julie Mowbray / Alamy p50; iStockPhoto.Richard Stanley p51; Galen Rowell / Mountain Light / Alamy p52; Getty Images / PhotoDisc p57; Icon / Ladd Co / Paramount / The Kobal Collection p70

Every effort has been made to contact copyright holders of material reproduced in this book. Any omissions will be rectified in subsequent printings if notice is given to the publishers.

Contents

Introduction **iv**

Developing reader **1**
Cycle A: Choosing and using reading strategies to understand and retrieve simple information from fiction texts 1
Cycle B: Choosing and using reading strategies to understand and retrieve simple information from non-fiction texts 7
Cycle C: Using reading strategies independently to retrieve information from fiction texts 13
Cycle D: Using reading strategies independently to retrieve information from non-fiction texts 19
Assessment cycle: Using reading strategies independently to retrieve information from texts 25

Secure developing reader **42**
Cycle A: Reading for meaning in fiction texts, supporting ideas with evidence from the text 42
Cycle B: Reading for meaning in non-fiction texts, supporting ideas with evidence from the text 48
Cycle C: Reading for meaning in fiction texts, supporting ideas with evidence from the text 54
Cycle D: Making judgements about texts, supported by evidence 60
Assessment cycle: Making judgements about texts, supporting ideas with evidence 66

Competent reader **86**
Cycle A: Using reading strategies to infer and deduce meaning in fiction texts 86
Cycle B: Choosing appropriate reading strategies 92
Cycle C: Making judgements about texts 98
Cycle D: Understanding the main purpose of a non-fiction text 104
Assessment cycle: Reading between the lines: consolidation and assessment 110

Secure competent reader **119**
Cycle A: To infer and deduce meanings supported by textual reference 119
Cycle B: To infer and deduce meaning in non-fiction texts, supported by evidence 125
Cycle C: Recognising a writer's point of view 131
Cycle D: To know how to identify and comment on writers' purposes and use of language 137
Assessment cycle: Consolidation and assessment 143

Teaching and assessing reading: some common problems and helpful strategies

Teaching reading in the secondary school poses a number of challenges:

- Reading is an 'invisible' process, something that we do 'in our heads', so that it can be a challenge for students and teachers to explain the nature of reading skills and to show how we get better at reading.
- It can be difficult to judge how much progress students are making as readers. For example, they often fail to transfer their reading skills from a supported classroom situation to independent reading, and they may be easily thrown by a more difficult or unfamiliar text.
- Writing produces permanent and tangible evidence for assessment. In contrast, evidence of reading ability is often ephemeral, glimpsed for example in students' answers to questions in class or during group discussions.
- Furthermore, assessing reading is difficult because we often rely on writing or speaking and listening as vehicles for students to show what they understand. If they are weak in these skills, students' real reading ability may not be seen.
- Anticipating the challenges that different students will face when reading is difficult because they are so varied and unpredictable, including factors such as level of interest in the topic or reading stamina when faced with longer texts.
- Once students can decode text, what does 'teaching reading' actually mean? What do we actively teach them and how do we plan for progression?

The following approaches should help students progress as readers:

- Model the thought processes involved in reading, and the use of strategies, for example through shared reading sessions where the teacher talks aloud about the process of reading and names the skills and strategies being applied. This will help students to see that reading is an active process rather than something we do silently and passively. Similarly, use vocabulary and imagery in the classroom that characterise reading as an active process, e.g. *investigate, explore, question, discover, search.*
- Many students learn effectively when ideas are presented visually and kinesthetically. It can help to make reading skills less abstract and more memorable for students by using symbol and action. Exploring ideas through drama and talk can also be very helpful.
- Help students transfer their skills by making explicit links between reading in English and reading in other subjects.
- Make reading social, collaborative and interactive as well as an individual, independent activity.
- Improve reading comprehension by actively teaching vocabulary.
- Teach students language for reflecting on their abilities as readers and involve them in self and peer assessment and target-setting.

The teaching approaches in this resource are designed to 'demystify' reading by:

- Forefronting in each lesson the thought processes involved in reading, making them clear to students through explicit teacher explanation and demonstration.
- Highlighting the reading strategies required to be successful readers, skills that are often invisible and therefore impenetrable for students unless explicitly explained and practised.
- Scaffolding students' learning to build confidence and stamina for working independently. Skills are explicitly taught by the teacher and trialled collaboratively with a partner, or in small groups, before students apply the skills independently.
- Using talk to strengthen students' understanding of reading processes and of their abilities as readers.

Research indicates that the single most important factor in improving reading comprehension is activating prior knowledge: students assimilate new information and process new vocabulary more effectively if they are able to link it to what they already know and establish a context for reading. Frequent use is made in this resource of questions, discussion prompts and explanations by students and the teacher. These have a vital role in activating students' thinking and showing them that reading is an active process of making meaning. Talk is also used widely to test understanding and to reflect on the skills that students are developing.

Many of the core principles of Assessment for Learning run through this reading resource, in particular:

- the sharing of easy-to-follow success criteria with students during peer and self-assessment sessions
- showing students the standards they are aiming for and the steps they need to take to get there
- encouraging students to reflect on their progress as readers and to set personal improvement targets.

Understanding Progression in Reading

It is essential for teachers to have a clear understanding of what constitutes progression in reading, in order to show groups of students and individuals what the next steps are in their learning. The following charts present pictures of progression in two different ways:

- Descriptive 'portraits' of readers at different points in their development as readers. These have been adapted from the Secondary National Strategy Progression Maps that are available as an online resource: www.standards.dfes.gov.uk/progressionmaps. You can use the portraits as a 'best-fit' checklist to help establish what your students can do and what they might struggle with, and to help you locate their attainment within the bigger picture of reading progression.
- Level-related criteria that detail features of attainment in each of the Assessment Focuses (AFs) for reading. These have been adapted from Assessing Pupils' Progress (APP) guidelines produced by the DfES and QCA, which provide a national standardised model for teacher assessment. They have been turned into student-speak so they can be shared easily with students, but retain sufficient detail to help teachers distinguish attainment within Levels 2, 3 and 4.

Point 1: Developing Reader

Reads with increasing fluency and accuracy and uses a range of strategies to construct meaning. These readers are beginning to:

- master the basic techniques of reading and develop greater fluency and accuracy
- use a range of strategies, including morphology, syntax or contextual cues to establish the meaning of an unfamiliar word
- increase the range of words that they recognise on sight
- develop the capacity to hear their errors and to self-correct
- move beyond decoding to read more purposefully for meaning
- engage with the literal meaning of straightforward texts, identify obvious points and make straightforward comments based on a single point of reference
- sometimes refer to parts of a text when answering a question.

Relevant targets for developing readers

1 Choose the best reading strategy to work out the meaning of words I do not know
2 Scan long sentences to make sure that I know where they end and how they are organised
3 Use at least two of the following reading strategies: questioning a text, making mental pictures based on what I read, predicting what might happen next in a text
4 Find information in the fiction and non-fiction texts I am reading.

Point 2: Secure Developing Reader

More secure developing readers have a growing range of strategies to support their reading and are able to apply them to longer and more complex texts. These readers:

- are increasingly confident in their choice of the most appropriate strategy to decode new and unfamiliar vocabulary
- can tackle extended sentences, often scanning ahead to see where they end and how they are structured
- are beginning to engage with the imaginative world of the fiction texts they encounter and take an interest in the range of information with which they are presented in non-fiction
- are beginning to play a more active role as readers, asking questions, speculating and making judgements, empathising and sympathising with characters and situations
- are able to identify some basic features of language and text organisation and also show some understanding of why a text has been written.

Relevant targets for secure developing readers

1 Find a quotation that could support my ideas
2 Skim and scan to find information quickly
3 Understand the connection between the purpose of a text and its layout and organisation
4 Use empathy to make judgements about a character.

Point 3: Competent Reader

Reads between the lines, seeing meaning that isn't stated directly. Deploys a wide range of active strategies to find and read texts for different purposes. These readers:

- have secured sufficient reading strategies, such as phonics, contextual cues, word attack skills and sense of grammar, to tackle new and unfamiliar texts with confidence, on their own
- may still read hesitantly on occasions, but possess sufficient self-help strategies to hear their errors and self-correct when necessary
- scan ahead to tackle longer, complex sentences
- are beginning to look beyond the sentence to paragraphs, chapters and whole-text layout
- are able to read for meaning and are willing participants in the imaginative world of the text
- visualise, empathise, and make judgements about what they read
- can find private reading a rewarding activity, worthy of the time and energy they invest in it
- can see what reading has to offer them.

Relevant targets for competent readers

1. Use clues from the text to work out what the writer means, even when it is not stated directly
2. Use a range of imaginative reading strategies when I read, such as speculation, prediction, questioning, empathy and visualisation
3. Find the main ideas in a text and support them with evidence
4. Explain why I like or dislike a text.

Point 4: Secure Competent Reader

Secure competent readers show understanding at a literal level and can also read beyond the text and between the lines. These readers:

- infer and deduce both hidden and implied meanings and, even though their inferences may not always be securely rooted in the text, they generally make sense
- deploy a range of imaginative responses to texts, such as empathy, prediction and speculation
- may compare the world of the text to their own experiences
- are able to make simple comments about a writer's viewpoint, as well as the effect of the text on the reader
- are able to pick out relevant points in both fiction and non-fiction texts, supporting them by some generally relevant textual reference or quotation
- can identify and make simple comments about the writer's use of language and organisational features.

Relevant targets for secure competent readers

1. Read between the lines to infer the writer's meaning
2. Make sure that I can find evidence in the text to support my inferences
3. Pick out and comment on some of the words chosen by the writer
4. Understand the writer's point of view in a text I am reading.

Assessment Focuses for Reading	If I'm Level 2 I can…	If I'm Level 3 I can…	If I'm Level 4 I can…
AF1 Use a range of strategies, including accurate decoding of text, to read for meaning.	• use different strategies to read unfamiliar words e.g. phonic knowledge, grammar and context clues • often notice when my reading does not make sense and take appropriate action e.g. self-correcting, looking back/forward or asking for meaning. • I may need help in choosing the best strategy for the text and task.	• use a range of reading strategies independently to tackle unfamiliar words and to establish meaning • usually choose an appropriate reading strategy for the text and the task.	• choose from a range of reading strategies and use them independently to read for meaning in a range of texts.
AF2 Understand, describe, select or retrieve information, events and ideas from texts and use quotation and reference to text.	• use different strategies to read unfamiliar words, e.g. phonic knowledge, grammar and context clues • scan text to locate specific details • identify and select the main ideas in texts • usually notice when my reading doesn't make sense and go back and correct it • read ahead to make sense of the whole sentence.	• use a range of reading strategies independently to tackle unfamiliar words • identify straightforward and more obvious points in texts although I sometimes misunderstand • quote from, or refer to, the text to back up my points although I don't always choose relevant evidence.	• identify some points that are relevant to the question or focus of discussion • support my comments with some generally relevant references to the text or quotations from it.
AF3 Deduce, infer or interpret information, events or ideas from texts.	• understand straightforward factual information in texts • understand main ideas in texts • recount main events or facts with some help • express an opinion or preference • find some details in the text in answer to specific questions.	• understand factual information and literal meanings in texts • try to read between the lines to find deeper meanings • make straightforward comments when talking about a text • give a personal view about a text • quote some details from the text or refer to information in it that supports my ideas..	• use evidence from different points in the text to read between the lines and show I understand what the writer means • make comments about the meaning of a text that are often correct but may not be rooted securely in the text or which fall back on repeating the story.

Assessment Focuses for Reading	If I'm Level 2 I can…	If I'm Level 3 I can…	If I'm Level 4 I can…
AF4 Identify and comment on the structure and organisation of texts, including grammatical and presentational features at word and sentence level.	• comment on some obvious features of the way information is presented, e.g. use of pictures, headlines and titles, and give simple reasons for their use • locate topic sentences • see how the main ideas are sequenced in a text.	• identify and comment on some straightforward features of presentation, e.g. headings, illustrations, subheadings • identify some of the ways in which the text is organised and structured, e.g. the order in which points are made; how the text begins and ends.	• identify some ways in which the text is organised and structured and make straightforward comments about why these features are used, e.g. bullet points to separate items in a list; use of headings to highlight key facts.
AF5 Explain and comment on writers' use of language, including grammatical and literary features at word and sentence level.	• locate specific words and phrases in answer to questions • read aloud with expression to show that I've understood the writer's intentions.	• identify a few straightforward features of the writer's use of language, although I might not add a comment about them, e.g. 'The writer uses lots of adjectives.'	• identify some basic features of a writer's use of language, e.g. 'all the questions make you want to find out what happens next' • make simple comments on the writer's choices, e.g. 'disgraceful is a good word to use to show he is upset.'
AF6 Identify and comment on writers' purposes and viewpoints, and the overall effect of the text on the reader.	• understand and comment on some simple features of the text such as the plot, characters or setting • identify the main purpose of the text and give simple reasons • express an opinion or preference about events and actions.	• identify and comment on the main purpose of the text and the writer's viewpoint, e.g. 'the writer doesn't like violence' • give a straightforward personal response to the text • express opinions and state preferences.	• identify the main purpose of the text, e.g. 'it's all about why going to the dentist is important and how you should look after your teeth' • make simple comments that show I'm aware of the writer's viewpoint and overall effect on the reader, e.g. 'he only tells you the good things about the theme park, which makes you want to visit it.'

Strategies and prompts for supporting developing readers

Reading is an active process of constructing the meaning of the text. Good readers make sense of what they read and are increasingly able to reflect on the implications of what the author has written. The ultimate purpose of reading is to understand and appreciate the writer's intentions and their craft so that a confident response can be made.

Slower readers usually find reading harder work and so require more encouragement. They need to gain confidence by reading familiar texts that they can access independently, and they will also need regular, supported practice in reading more challenging, unfamiliar texts. Although it might be tempting to try and speed up the process by reading these texts for them, this will not in the long run help them to become independent, active readers. Developing readers will need to be taught, or reminded of, a range of strategies that will help them work out meaning by themselves.

When you listen to students read and they become 'stuck', use an appropriate prompt from the list below to encourage active, independent use of strategies.

- **Try reading from the beginning of the sentence again and think what would fit.**

  Encourage insecure readers to re-read as a first strategy. Re-reading helps focus the reader on understanding and constructing meaning more than other strategies.

- **What does your word begin with? Think of a word that looks right and makes sense.**

  Encourage the student to attend to visual information such as the significant letters of the word, to link this visual information with known items, and to cross-check with meaning.

- **Does that make sense and sound right?**

  Encourage the student to use meaning and structure to confirm.

- **How can you be sure? or How do you know?**

  Encourage the student to take responsibility for confirmation.

- **Does that make sense and look right to you?**

  Encourage the student to cross-check meaning and visual information.

- **Would you read that again?**

  Encourage the student to check further, putting the word back into context and perhaps self-correct.

- **What's another word that begins with those two letters? Let's write some down.**

  Refer to what the student finds familiar in another context.

Strategies and prompts for supporting competent readers

The most appropriate strategies will depend on the kind of text and the purpose for which it is being read, but it is always worth encouraging active reading through the use of reflective questions such as these:

Before I start

- Why am I reading this text?
- What kind of text is it?
- What do I expect it to contain/be about? Do I need to read it closely or should I skim it for basic meaning or scan it to locate the relevant part?

Words

- Why has the writer used that particular word?
- I'm not sure what that word means: what's my best guess after looking at what comes before and what follows?
- Do I recognise the meaning of part of the word?

Sentences

- Do I need to go back and read that long sentence again? Does it make sense now? If not, can I see what is the subject and the main verb?
- Why is the writer using these long/short sentences?

Paragraphs

- What is the topic sentence of this paragraph?
- If I had to give this paragraph a title, what would it be?

Meaning of the whole text

- Are there any connectives that show me how ideas are linked in this text?
- Does this piece present itself in the usual way for a text of this type or does it do things differently?
- What other writing does it remind me of, or contrast with?
- Is there any other meaning 'between the lines' that I have to work out for myself?
- What is the character thinking or feeling? What would I think or feel if I were them?
- What does the writer want me to think at this point?
- Would people at that time in history/in that society have had ideas/thoughts/feelings that were different from mine?

Evaluation

- Why do I like/dislike what I am reading? Do I agree with the writer's point of view?
- Can I find words, phrases or sentences in the text that are clear evidence for what I think?

Using running records to assess students' reading

A 'running record' or 'miscue analysis' is a form of reading assessment that allows you to see what reading strategies a student is using so that you can plan for teaching those strategies which will increase the student's ability to decode and understand what they read.

Typically, running reading records:

- are carried out on a section of 100 words from a text; it could be a story the student is currently reading
- avoid the potential stress of a test situation
- can show whether a text is at an appropriate level for a student: this may be especially useful with a textbook the student may be using in a particular curriculum area
- can provide information about the student's particular difficulty, and thus how best to help.

Because it is diagnostic and formative, a running record can be more useful than a test that produces a reading age, but offers no suggestions as to how to intervene to move the student on.

Who best can administer a running record?

The assessment can be done by:

- teachers
- teaching assistants
- librarians
- paired reading volunteers, e.g. older students/6th-formers
- parents.

In preparation you will need either:

- a photocopy of the page to be read by the student, or
- a transparent sheet that can be placed over your copy of the text.

What to do

- Ask the student to read the passage aloud in her/his own time.
- As the student reads, mark any errors on the photocopy or the acetate sheet using the system and symbols explained below.
- If the student hesitates for too long and plainly cannot proceed, give the word and note the fact on the record sheet: see 'hesitation' below.
- If the student pauses continuously and cannot get any sense of the text, it is too difficult for her/him and another text should be chosen.
- Once the text has been finished, thank the student and praise the reading.
- After the test, the type and number of errors can be examined to see if any patterns emerge.

Explanations of errors and symbols to use in miscue analysis

Refusal	The student does not read the word or any part of it	_ _ _ _ _ _ _
Self-correction	The student reads the word incorrectly at first but then corrects	Write 'error' above word then 'SC'
Omission	The student misses the word out	Circle the word
Insertion	The student adds a word/words that are not in the text	^
Reversal	The word is reversed, most frequently with small words such as *saw* for *was*	'S' on its side
Hesitation	The student clearly hesitates while decoding a word **but note**: it is important to allow the student time to read or self-correct before the adult intervenes or corrects	H or /
Substitution	An incorrect word is substituted for the word in the passage	Cross out misread word and write substituted word above

What can we learn from the mistakes and what strategies need to be taught?

- Does the substituted word make sense in the **passage** being read?

  YES: the student can use cues from the meaning of the passage (semantic cues).

  NO: the student has not learned that reading should make sense. Some poor readers concentrate so much on the decoding of words that they lose the meaning.

  Possible teaching strategy: paired or shared reading followed by discussion about the text's meaning.

- Does the substituted word make sense in the **sentence** being read?

  YES: the student understands the language of the sentence (uses syntactic cues).

  NO: the student has not learned that the structure of the sentence limits the possible correct responses.

  Possible teaching strategies: prediction exercises and cloze procedures.

- Does the substituted word look and sound like the original word?

  YES: the student can use print cues (phonographic cues).

  NO: the student's word attack skills are insecure.

  Possible teaching strategies: a structured phonographic teaching programme; using questions that direct the student to looking, e.g. 'what does the word begin with', 'can you see any smaller words you recognise?'

A simple way of reaching judgements about the suitability of text

- If 95% or more of the words are read correctly, the student can clearly read this level without help.
- If 90–95% of the words are read correctly, the student will need help to make full use of a passage at this level: this is the correct level for guided reading and reading tuition.
- If less than 90% correct, the passage is too difficult and an easier one should be found.

In addition:

- It is sometimes useful to have some prepared questions that tackle both literal and inferential comprehension to check whether a student understands what is read. It is better if the teacher prepares these and they are kept for future use.
- If there is little comprehension, then the student needs to be prepared to read by discussing the context and content, e.g. from pictures or teacher prompts.
- The student then needs to have her/his attention drawn to sentences and words that develop the context and content and convey first the literal meaning and then the inferred meaning.
- This can be done through careful questioning and directing students to find the answer in specific sentences or sections of the text.
- Once the meaning has been understood, the tutor needs to return to the text as a whole and discuss the context and content and remind the student how and where the detail comes.

Developing Reader: point 1 on the progression map (Level 2c–2b)

Cycle A Fiction Level 2c

Progression map target areas
Target area 1: Choosing appropriate reading strategies
Target area 2: Scanning ahead to work out the structure of extended sentences
Target area 4: Reading for meaning to retrieve information from fiction texts

Overall learning objective for Cycle A (three lessons)
- Choosing and using reading strategies to understand and retrieve simple information from fiction texts

Lessons 1–3 learning objectives
- to know how to use phonic strategies to read unfamiliar words
- to be able to use knowledge of grammar and context to read for meaning
- to be able to recount the main events in a fiction text
- to be able to understand the main ideas in a fiction text

Outline of activities in the three lessons
- Introduce and practise use of searchlights model for reading.
- Introduce and use key question prompts highlighting strategies used for reading unfamiliar texts.
- Model using the strategies on short fiction texts and poems.
- Use sequencing activities to establish main events of a narrative.
- Use description and storytelling to help students understand main ideas, engage with text, predict and speculate.

Cycle B Non-Fiction Level 2c

Progression map target areas
Target area 1: Choosing appropriate reading strategies
Target area 2: Scanning ahead to work out the structure of extended sentences
Target area 4: Reading for meaning to retrieve information from non-fiction texts

Overall learning objective for Cycle B (three lessons)
- Choosing and using reading strategies to understand and retrieve simple information from non-fiction texts

Lessons 4–6 learning objectives
- to know how to use phonic strategies to read unfamiliar words
- to know how to use knowledge of phonics, grammar and context to read for meaning
- to be able to recount the main facts in a non-fiction text
- to be able to comment on obvious features of the text

Outline of activities in the three lessons
- Practise using reading strategies to establish meaning of words taken from non-fiction text. Predict main ideas in text.
- Model how to highlight key words, points and phrases within a simple text to identify simple, obvious, key points.
- Model how to use *who, what, why, where* and *when* questions to find specific and relevant information, e.g.:
  - o Who was involved? (Look for a name, a proper noun, etc.)
  - o What happened? (Scan for an event of action, a verb.)
  - o Where did it happen? (Look for a place name, a capital letter.)

- When did it happen? (Scan for numbers, dates and time, e.g. a.m./p.m.)
- Why did it happen? (Read more closely. Support ideas with a brief quotation.)

- Ask students to match illustrations to appropriate sections of a text.
- Investigate key features of layout of simple non-fiction texts.

Cycle C Fiction Level 2c–2b

Progression map target areas
Target area 2: Scanning ahead to work out the structure of extended sentences
Target area 3: Using active reading strategies
Target area 4: Reading for meaning to retrieve information from fiction texts

Overall learning objective for Cycle C
- Using reading strategies independently to read for meaning in fiction texts.

Lessons 7–9 learning objectives
- to be able to extract information from fiction texts
- to be able to use punctuation cues when reading for meaning and read ahead in the text
- to recognise when meaning does not make sense and be able to self-correct or problem-solve
- to be able to comment on how information is presented in a text

Outline of activities in the three lessons
- Read aloud or use a story tape to provide students with good models of the way intonation and pause can be used to draw out the meaning of an extended sentence.
- Introduce and practise using active reading strategies to establish overall meaning in a text: visualising, questioning, predicting and speculating.
- Teach 'sentence attack' skills. Remind students about skimming and scanning, then model how to scan ahead to the end of a long sentence to see where it ends. Point out any helpful end punctuation, such as a question mark or exclamation mark. Give students two or three examples to try out in pairs.
- Model how to find the main clause in a complex sentence. Underline the main clause, demonstrating to students how they can strip a long, complex sentence back to its bare bones in order to identify its basic meaning.
- Rewrite a long, complex sentence as a series of short sentences and draw out the differences.
- Rewrite a long, complex sentence in a visual format, showing how other parts relate to the main clause.
- Ask and answer questions about events, characters and settings in fiction texts.
- Make predictions about characters and actions, based on evidence from the text.

Cycle D Non-Fiction Level 2c–2b

Progression map target areas
Target area 2: Scanning ahead to work out the structure of extended sentences
Target area 3: Using active reading strategies
Target area 4: Reading for meaning to retrieve information from non-fiction texts

Overall learning objective for Cycle D
- Using reading strategies independently to retrieve information from non-fiction texts

Lessons 10–12 learning objectives
- to be able to use punctuation cues when reading for meaning and read ahead in the text
- to recognise when meaning does not make sense and be able to self-correct or problem-solve
- to be able to extract information from simple non-fiction texts
- to be able to comment on how information is presented in a text

Outline of activities in the three lessons

- Read aloud to model how to use intonation and pause to draw out meaning from complex sentences.
- Introduce and practise using active reading strategies to establish overall meaning in a text: visualising, questioning, predicting and speculating.
- Teach 'sentence attack' skills. Remind students about skimming and scanning, then model how to scan ahead to the end of a long sentence to see where it ends. Point out any helpful end punctuation, such as a question mark or exclamation mark.
- Ask students to use a QUADs grid to investigate and make notes on a non-fiction text:
  1. **Q**uestion
  2. **A**nswer
  3. **D**etail
  4. Two are better than one, because they have a good return for their work: ource
- Model how to use 5W questions to scan a text and extract information from it.
- Introduce and practise using vocabulary to describe presentational devices used in non-fiction texts.
- Sequence main ideas in texts; use clues to make predictions about content and order of information.

Cycle E Consolidation and Assessment Level 2b

Progression map target areas
Target area 4: Reading for meaning to retrieve information from texts

Lessons 13–15 learning objective
- to know how to use reading strategies independently to retrieve information from fiction and non-fiction texts

The Assessment Task will test students' ability to:
- choose the best reading strategy to work out the meaning of unfamiliar words
- scan long sentences to make sure they know where they end and how they are organised
- use at least two of the following reading strategies: questioning a text, making mental pictures based on what is read, predicting what might happen next in a text
- find information in fiction and non-fiction texts.

Outline of activities in the three lessons
- Recap previous main learning points.
- Introduce Assessment Task.
- Guided preparation.
- Self/peer/teacher assessment of task.
- Next steps target-setting.

Secure Developing Reader: point 2 on the progression map (Level 2b–2a)

Cycle A Fiction Level 2b–2a

Progression map target areas
Target area 1: Finding and using textual reference
Target area 2: Skimming and scanning
Target area 3: Understanding text layout and organisation

Overall learning objective for Cycle A (three lessons)
- Reading for meaning in fiction texts and supporting ideas with evidence from the text

Lessons 1–3 learning objectives

- to be able to read simple unfamiliar texts accurately
- to know how to scan a text to locate relevant information and read ahead independently
- to know how to use expression and intonation to enhance meaning when reading
- to be able to give a balanced retelling of a story and to retell clearly
- to be able to comment on a story's main characters using evidence from the text

Outline of activities in the three lessons

- Read aloud fluently and with expression, e.g. to highlight characterisation.
- Model use of reading strategies to establish overall meaning: visualising, questioning, predicting and speculating.
- Introduce empathising as a reading strategy: model how to make judgements on characters, using empathy question prompts.
- Plot main events and actions to show narrative structure. Use to retell a story in sequence.
- Ask key questions about a text and use them to scan for information, e.g. about characters.

Cycle B Non-Fiction Level 2b–2a

Progression map target areas

Target area 1: Finding and using textual reference
Target area 2: Skimming and scanning
Target area 3: Understanding text layout and organisation
Target area 4: Using empathy to make judgements

Overall learning objective for Cycle B (three lessons)

- Reading for meaning in non-fiction texts and supporting ideas with evidence from the text

Lessons 4–6 learning objectives

- to be able to read simple unfamiliar texts accurately
- to know how to scan a text to locate relevant information and read ahead independently
- to be able to tackle unfamiliar words and be aware of strategies used to do this
- to be able to extract information from non-fiction text in answer to specific questions

Outline of activities in the three lessons

- Read aloud fluently and with expression, e.g. to highlight main facts and opinions.
- Model use of reading strategies to establish overall meaning: visualising, questioning, predicting and speculating.
- Introduce empathising as a reading strategy: model how to make judgements on ideas in non-fiction texts, using empathy question prompts, e.g. to help activate prior knowledge about a topic.
- Model how to highlight key words, points and phrases within a simple text to identify simple, obvious, key points.
- Sequence events in the correct order

Cycle C Fiction Level 2b–2a

Progression map target areas

Target area 1: Finding and using textual reference
Target area 2: Using empathy to make judgements

Overall learning objective for Cycle C

- Making judgements about characters, ideas and events in fiction texts, supported by evidence from the text

Lessons 7–9 learning objectives

- to be able to give a balanced retelling of a story and retell clearly
- to be able to respond to questions about feelings created by the story
- to be able to comment on a story's main characters using evidence from the text

- to know how to comment on some of the ways in which a text is written or presented
- to be able to respond to questions that invite speculation and prediction
- to be able to express an opinion about the events or actions of a story
- to know how to use expression and intonation to enhance meaning when reading

Outline of activities in the three lessons
- Highlight and practise using reading strategies to search for meaning in fiction texts: visualising, empathising, predicting and speculating, questioning
- Use shared reading to model the way a reader questions a text
- Model use of sentence stems for speculation such as: *I wonder whether…perhaps it might…maybe it is…it could be…*
- Encourage students to predict what might happen next at key points in a text, with reasons why. Compare predictions with what actually happens
- Use labelled drawings as prompts to tell a story

Cycle D Non-Fiction Level 2b–2a

Progression map target areas
Target area 1: Finding and using textual reference
Target area 2: Understanding text layout and organisation
Target area 3: Using empathy to make judgements

Overall learning objective for Cycle D
- Making judgements about texts, supported by evidence

Lessons 10–12 learning objectives
- to know how to scan for and locate relevant information in answer to specific questions
- to be able to extract information from a non-fiction text for a specific purpose
- to know how to comment on some of the ways in which a text is written or presented
- to be able to express opinions and make judgements

Outline of activities in the three lessons
- Highlight and practise using reading strategies to search for meaning in non-fiction texts: visualising, empathising, predicting and speculating, questioning.
- Use shared reading to focus on punctuation for meaning.
- Summarise and sequence main ideas in a text; predict how a text will end.
- Use vocabulary and prompts to highlight key features of presentation and layout, supported by examples.
- Model how to annotate a text to highlight its organisational features, e.g. sub-headings, diagrams, paragraphs, bold typeface.
- Model how to use text layout to help navigate a text and find answers to questions.

Cycle E Consolidation and Assessment Level 2a

Assessment Task will test students' ability to:
- Find a quotation to support ideas
- Skim and scan to find information quickly
- Use empathy to make judgements about a character

Overall learning objective for cycle E
- Make judgements about texts, supporting ideas with evidence

Lessons 13–15 learning objectives
- To know how to scan for and locate relevant information in answer to specific questions
- To be able to extract information from a text for a specific purpose

- To be able to express an opinion about a text

To cover in the three lessons
- Recap previous main learning points.
- Introduce Assessment Task.
- Guided preparation.
- Self/peer/teacher assessment of task.
- Next steps target-setting.

Competent Reader: point 3 on the progression map (Level 3c–3b)

Cycle A Fiction Level 3c

Progression map target areas
Target area 1: Reading between the lines
Target area 2: Using a range of reading strategies

Overall learning objective for Cycle A (three lessons)
- Using reading strategies to infer and deduce meaning in fiction texts

Lessons 1–3 learning objectives
- to understand that some meanings are literal and some meanings are non-literal
- to be able to select relevant information in a text
- to be able to draw conclusions about meaning
- to be able to link details in a text in order to make a deduction
- to be able to use a range of reading strategies to access meaning
- to be able to draw conclusions about reading

Outline of activities in the three lessons
- Recap use of reading strategies (cards: visualising, empathising, speculating and predicting, asking questions).
- Introduce 'iceberg of meaning': use first on an image, then texts.
- Activities to practise inference and deduction using fiction texts linked by theme. Skills targeted:
  - use clues from the text to work out what the writer means even when it is not stated directly
  - use a range of imaginative reading strategies when reading, such as speculation, prediction, questioning, empathy and visualisation
  - find the main ideas in a text and support them with evidence
  - next steps needed to get better at the learning objectives

Cycle B Non-Fiction Level 3c

Progression map target areas
Target area 2: Using a range of reading strategies
Target area 3: Finding the main ideas in a text and supporting them with evidence

Overall learning objective for Cycle B (three lessons)
- Choosing appropriate reading strategies

Lessons 4–6 learning objectives
- to know how to skim a text for its general meaning
- to be able to select information relevant to a question or task
- to be able to put information from a text into own words

Outline of activities in the three lessons
- Learning new reading strategy: skimming and scanning..
- Sorting relevant from non-relevant information for a particular task.
- Summarising information in own words.

Cycle C Fiction Level 3c–3b

Progression map target areas
Target area 1: Reading between the lines
Target area 2: Using a range of reading strategies
Target area 4: Explaining and justifying textual preference

Overall learning objective for Cycle C
- Using reading strategies independently to infer and deduce meaning from fiction texts; making judgements about texts

Lessons 7–9 learning objectives
- to be able to infer and deduce meaning from texts
- to be able to use inference to predict and speculate
- to be able to comment on evidence found in a text
- to be able to express personal preferences about texts

Outline of activities in the three lessons
- Consolidating reading strategies, adding next step skills: passing comments/making judgements; looking forwards and backwards; predicting based on evidence
- Using iceberg model to uncover layers of meaning in texts
- Comparing ideas in texts and expressing a preference
- Extending the use of 5W questions to include 'how'
- Beginning to focus attention on the language of text

Cycle D Non-Fiction Level 3c–3b

Progression map target areas
Target area 2: Using a range of reading strategies
Target area 3: Finding the main ideas in a text and supporting them with evidence
Target area 4: Explaining and justifying textual preference

Overall learning objective for Cycle D
- Using reading strategies independently to infer and deduce meaning from non-fiction texts; making judgements about texts

Lessons 10–12 learning objectives
- to be able to understand the main purpose of a text
- to be able to find information from a text independently
- to be able to categorise information into groups
- to be able to recognise basic organisation and presentational features of texts

Outline of activities in the three lessons
- Considering the purpose of texts
- Activities investigating the structure and organisation of a text
- Commenting on effectiveness of images, words, phrases and whole texts on the reader

Cycle E Consolidation and Assessment Level 3b

Lessons 13–15 learning objective

- To be able to use a range of reading strategies to infer and deduce meaning in fiction and/or non-fiction texts

Assessment Task will test students' ability to:
- use clues from the text to work out what the writer means, even when it is not stated directly
- use a range of imaginative reading strategies, such as speculation, prediction, questioning, empathy and visualisation
- find the main ideas in a text and support them with evidence
- explain why they like or dislike a text.

To cover in the three lessons
- Recap previous main learning points
- Introduce Assessment Task
- Guided preparation
- Self/peer/teacher assessment of task
- Next steps target-setting ideas
- Active learning approaches to engage with the text

Secure competent reader: point 4 on the progression map (Level 3b–3a)

Cycle A Fiction Level 3b–3a

Progression map target areas
Target area 1: Inference and deduction
Target area 2: Using textual evidence to support inference

Overall learning objective for Cycle A (three lessons)
- To infer and deduce meanings which are supported by textual evidence

Lessons 1–3 learning objectives
- to be able to use inference to predict and speculate, especially about characters and actions
- to be able to deduce meaning from a text
- to be able to comment on the writer's use of vocabulary
- to be able to annotate a text, making notes for later use

Outline of activities in the three lessons
- Learning how to make successful notes, using them afterwards
- Active approaches to engaging with a wider choice of vocabulary
- Learning how to quote evidence
- Building comments about language use and meaning, e.g. single-word analysis

Cycle B Non-Fiction Level 3b–3a

Progression map target areas
Target area 1: Inference and deduction
Target area 2: Using textual evidence to support inference

Overall learning objective for Cycle B (three lessons)
- To infer and deduce meanings which are supported by textual evidence

Lessons 4–6 learning objectives
- to be able to confidently retrieve and confirm simple facts

- to be able to independently record the findings of research undertaken
- to be able to identify some organisational and presentational features of texts
- to know how to identify features of the writer's use of language

Outline of activities in the three lessons

- Scanning for facts in answer to specific questions.
- Close reading text to confirm or refute facts.
- Note-making to record findings, e.g. using a for-and-against grid or a Venn diagram.
- Vocabulary and prompts for identifying features of language use, including layout.
- Learning how to make notes to record research findings
- Further investigation of the way that texts are structured
- Researching using more than one text

Cycle C Fiction Level 3a

Progression map target areas
Target area 3: Identifying and commenting on a writer's choice of language
Target area 4: Understanding the writer's viewpoint

Overall learning objective for Cycle C
- To understand a writer's viewpoint

Lessons 7–9 learning objectives
- to be able to support comments about a text with mainly relevant quotations from or references to the text
- to understand how to paraphrase or retell, to support comment
- to be able to make some comments about the effects and purpose of a writer's choice of language
- To understand a writer's viewpoint

Outline of activities in the three lessons
- Learning to paraphrase
- Annotating text and explaining writers' effects.
- Extending comments about features of the text, by beginning to use PEE paragraphs
- Responding to the viewpoint of images and texts

Cycle D Non-Fiction Level 3a

Progression map target areas
Target area 3: Identifying and commenting on a writer's choice of language
Target area 4: Understanding the writer's viewpoint

Overall learning objective for Cycle D
- To be able to comment on a writer's viewpoint

Lessons 10–12 learning objectives
- to be able to support comments about a text with mainly relevant quotations from or references to the text
- to understand how to paraphrase or retell, to support comment
- to be able to make some comments about the effects and purposes of a writer's choice of language
- to know how to carry out research using several sources
- understanding how a writer's language reveals viewpoint

Outline of activities in the three lessons
- Matching statements about a text to evidence from it
- Summing up information in own words
- Finding and comparing information from two or more texts
- Building comments about effectiveness of language beginning to use PEE
- Building to us independence in making and supporting comments about a text

Cycle E Consolidation and Assessment Level 3a

Lessons 13–15 learning objectives
- to comment on writers' viewpoints and choice of language in different texts

Assessment Task will test students' ability to:
- to be able to independently select reading skills to decipher meaning
- read between the lines to infer the writer's meaning
- find evidence in the text to support inferences
- pick out and comment on some of the words chosen by the writer

- understand the writer's point of view

To cover in the three lessons

- Recap main learning points
- Preparation for Assessment Task
- Self/peer/teacher assessment
- Next steps target-setting

Choosing and using reading strategies to understand and retrieve simple information from fiction texts

Developing reader

Cycle A

Duration: 1 hour

Resources needed	Lesson aims	Assessment Focuses
• CD-ROM Cycle A (Developing reader) resource sheets 1.1 and 1.2: tongue-twisters starter and extracts from 'Jabberwocky' to cut up and use with projector • Student Book pages 6–9: explanation of how we use our brain to think and read; prompts for reading unfamiliar texts • Student Book pages 10–11: illustration of Jabberwock and context questions	• to know how to use phonic strategies to read unfamiliar words • to be able to use knowledge of grammar and context to read for meaning **Target areas** • Target area 1: Choosing appropriate reading strategies • Target area 4: Reading for meaning to retrieve information from fiction texts	AF1, AF2, AF8

Starter (15 minutes)

Use the tongue-twisters on resource sheet 1.1 to practise hearing and saying blended sounds at the start and end of words, concentrating on the phonemes *sh, ch, ck*. Get students to make up their own tongue-twisters using the same phonemes. They can mix real and invented words that contain these sounds. Encourage students to say the tongue-twisters in different ways, e.g. in a whisper, loudly, in pairs at the same speed, but make sure you can hear every word clearly.

Introduction (15 minutes)

Using pages 8–9 of the Student Book, discuss with students the different skills and strategies we use when we read (graphic and phonic clues; knowledge of grammar and context). Explain that they will be practising these skills in the next few lessons as they read different texts that are connected by the theme of giants and monsters.

Using pages 10–11 of the Student Book, look together at the illustration from the poem 'Jabberwocky' and the questions that go with it. Explain to the students that you want them to think about the picture's meaning by asking questions that will explore its context. Read the context questions one at a time; give students 30 seconds to decide an answer with a partner. When all the questions have been answered, briefly discuss as a group: 'What do we know for sure? What are we less certain about?'

Development (20 minutes)

Explain that the picture shows characters from a famous poem by Lewis Carroll. The students' task is to decide which part of the poem is shown in the illustration. Using resource sheet 1.2 (extracts from the poem cut into strips), display each extract in turn, reading them aloud as you do so. After each extract, give students 30 seconds to decide if it is the best match for the illustration. Take feedback, encouraging the students to give reasons for their choice. Ask again: 'What do we know for sure? What are we less certain about?'

Remind the students of the different 'searchlight' strategies for reading and how they have just been using context clues to make meaning. Explain that they are now going to practise phonic skills and using knowledge of grammar to read for meaning.

Display all the strips from the poem in the correct order and read them aloud, slowly and with expression. The students decide which words they already know and which words are unfamiliar. Taking their suggestions, highlight known words in one colour and unfamiliar words in another. Model how to use phonic knowledge to read some of the unfamiliar words, e.g. *Jabberwock, vorpal, manxome, whiffling, tulgey, galumphing*. Split the words into syllables and say them in turn. Highlight the phonemes in the final syllable of *Jabberwock:* w/o/ck*;* show the separate phonemes and then blend them together to read the word. Together, list other words the students know that have the same vowel phoneme and end with the *ck* phoneme, e.g. *sock, clock, flock, stock, shock*. Do the same for another word, e.g. highlighting the *wh* phoneme in *whiffling* and listing other words that start with

Choosing and using reading strategies to understand and retrieve simple information from fiction texts

Developing reader

Cycle A

Duration: 1 hour

it: *what, which, where,* etc.

Read the last two strips again and ask what kinds of words *whiffling* and *galumphing* are. Decide together which verbs in 'real English' might replace them. Draw attention to the *-ing* ending, which shows that the words are verbs.

Give time for students in pairs to decide 'real English' meanings for the adjectives *vorpal* (sword) and *tulgey* (wood). Invite them to look back at the picture to help them decide. Take suggestions and vote on the best.

Plenary (10 minutes)

Read the whole poem to the students, slowly and with expression. Ask them to raise a hand every time they hear a word that rhymes with a word that has gone before. At the end, ask them to say aloud the words from the poem that they most easily remember.

Extension activity

The students' task is to learn any two lines of the poem by heart and to practise saying them aloud, clearly and with expression.

Lesson Plan
2 of 3

Choosing and using reading strategies to understand and retrieve simple information from fiction texts

Developing reader

Cycle A

Duration: 1 hour

Resources needed	Lesson aims	Assessment Focuses
• large three-phoneme frame drawn on whiteboard, i.e. [ ] [ ] [ ] • mini-whiteboards, one per pupil; markers and wipers • projector • CD-ROM Cycle A (Developing reader) resource sheet 2.1: extracts from *The Iron Man* on whiteboard and card • Student Book page 12: *The Iron Man* text	• to know how to use phonic strategies to read unfamiliar words • to be able to use knowledge of grammar and context to read for meaning • to be able to recount the main events in a fiction text • to be able to understand the main ideas in a fiction text **Target areas** • Target area 1: Choosing appropriate reading strategies • Target area 2: Scanning ahead to work out the structure of extended sentences • Target area 4: Reading for meaning to retrieve information from fiction texts	AF1, AF2, AF8

Starter (15 minutes)

The aim of this activity is to practise hearing and saying the separate phonemes in short words. Explain that every word we say is made up of one or more sounds that blend together when we say it. Being able to separate the different sounds and checking they have used the right letter combinations that make those sounds will help the students' spelling. We call this segmenting. Being able to join the different sounds together quickly to say the word will help students' reading. We call this blending. Using the phoneme frame on the board to demonstrate, say some simple three-phoneme words, writing them into the frame as you say them, e.g. *pen*: p/e/n; *mug*: m/u/g; *lid*: l/i/d. Check that students are clear about the terms 'vowel' and 'consonant'. Say the following words and ask the students to write on their whiteboards, and hold up each time, the number of phonemes (separate sounds) they can hear: *chip, shop, dish, bell, tick* (the answer is three in each case). Write *chip* in the phoneme frame on the board: ch/i/p. Explain that some phonemes (sounds) are represented by more than one letter, e.g. *ch, sh, th, ck.* Show the students an example drawn in the frame, e.g. *dish:* d/i/sh. Get them to draw a three-phoneme frame on their mini-whiteboards. Read the following words one at a time, pausing while the students write each word in their frame and hold them up to show each time: *rush*: r/u/sh; *push*: p/u/sh; *thin*: th/i/n; *shut*: sh/u/t; *chap*: ch/a/p; *sock*: s/o/ck. Correct any errors, demonstrating on the teacher's whiteboard.

Introduction (15 minutes)

Using pages 8–9 in the Student Book, remind the students of the different 'searchlights' we use when we read (graphic and phonic clues; knowledge of grammar and context). Explain that they will practise using all these strategies to explore the meaning of a text, starting with some extracts from it. Using resource sheet 2. 1 Set A (whiteboard strips) project them onto the whiteboard one at a time, students reading each one aloud. When all the strips are displayed, ask: 'Who or what is being described here?' Give the students 30 seconds to decide, then take suggestions, encouraging explanations of the clues they are using to decide (some may recognise details from *The Iron Man* if they have encountered this text before).

Displaying one strip at a time, practise sentence-building with the students by writing in a subject and a verb and appropriate punctuation to make a complete sentence. Use the same subject each time – *The man* – and ask the students to suggest a suitable verb. Show them how they can vary the position of the subject and verb in the sentence. Get them to read each completed sentence aloud, then the whole text when complete, for example: *The man seemed taller than a house. At the top of the cliff, the man sat down. The man's eyes shone like headlamps. Shaped like a dustbin, the man's head was huge. Hearing the sea, the man turned towards it.* Ask: 'Who might this person be? Where might he

Choosing and using reading strategies to understand and retrieve simple information from fiction texts

Developing reader

Cycle A

Duration: 1 hour

have come from?' Allow one minute for discussion, then take suggestions.

Development (20 minutes)

Write the word *iron* on the whiteboard and pronounce it with the students. Remind them that it can be used as a noun (a type of metal, a household object) and as an adjective (e.g. iron railings), which is how you want them to use it now. Ask them to put *iron* in front of *man* in each sentence and read aloud the whole text. Ask: 'Who do we think this person is now? Where might he have come from and why?'

Direct the students to pages 12–13 of the Student Book. Ask them to look at the cover of *The Iron Man* and describe what they can see. Ask pairs of students to decide an answer to the question: 'Is this what you expected the Iron Man to look like or not?' Combine pairs into groups of four and compare answers. Briefly take feedback.

Read the 'Ask yourself' questions on page 12 of the Student Book with the students. In pairs, they should answer the questions orally, then join another pair to compare answers. Briefly discuss as a whole class answers to questions 3 and 4. Encourage the students to make links with other stories they know about creatures from other worlds that they might draw on to predict and speculate.

Plenary (10 minutes)

Project the strips from resource sheet 2.1 (Set A as used before) on the whiteboard in random order. Ask groups of three or four students to use the strips as prompts to tell the story of the Iron Man's arrival on Earth. Their challenge is to keep speaking for at least a minute, adding their own details to fill out the story. Hear two or three versions.

Extension activity

Give the students the following to learn as a tongue-twister:

The Iron Man's huge iron ears slowly turned.

Lesson Plan 3 of 3

Choosing and using reading strategies to understand and retrieve simple information from fiction texts

Developing reader

Cycle A

Duration: 1 hour

Resources needed

- large four-phoneme frame drawn on whiteboard, i.e.

- plain A4 paper and pencils, one per group of three or four
- Student Book pages 12–13: *The Iron Man* book cover
- CD-ROM Cycle A (Developing reader) resource sheet 2.1: Set B cut-up strips, set of cards per pair and whiteboard strips for teacher's use

Lesson aims

- to know how to use phonic strategies to read unfamiliar words
- to be able to use knowledge of grammar and context to read for meaning
- to be able to recount the main events in a fiction text
- to be able to understand the main ideas in a fiction text

Target areas

- Target area 1: Choosing appropriate reading strategies
- Target area 2: Scanning ahead to work out the structure of extended sentences
- Target area 4: Reading for meaning to retrieve information from fiction texts

Assessment Focuses

AF1, AF2, AF8

Starter (15 minutes)

Gather the students round the whiteboard. Write the word *lap* in the four-phoneme frame, leaving the first box free. Isolate the phonemes and then blend them to read the word. Write *c* in the first box: isolate the phonemes: c/l/a/p and then blend to read the word: *clap*. Ask the students if they can suggest a different letter for the first frame that will make a new word. Show s/l/a/p; f/l/a/p, segmenting each phoneme and then blending to read the word. Now write the word *rush* in the last three frames: r/u/sh. Check that the students have remembered that a phoneme (one sound) may be made up of more than one letter, e.g. *sh*, *ch*, *th*, *ck* (these are called digraphs). Write *b* in the first box and isolate the phonemes: b/r/u/sh, then blend to read the word: *brush*. Rub out the *b* and ask a student to write the letter *c* in the first frame, a second student to sound out the separate phonemes and a third to blend and read the word: *crush*. Repeat with different examples, asking for students' suggestions to build and change words from given starter phonemes that you write into the frame. Examples are below (starter phonemes in bold).

th		**n**		thin, than, then, think, thank
	l		**sh**	lush, lash, flesh, flash, flush (change l to r for rash, fresh)
	l		**ck**	lock, clock, lack, black, block, luck
		s	**t**	chest, best, bust, mast, most, mist, last, etc.

Introduction (15 minutes)

Explain the emphasis on using a range of strategies to read for meaning which the students will be trying out on a longer extract from *The Iron Man*.

Organise the students in groups of three or four and give each group a sheet of plain A4 paper and a pencil. One student turns to pages 12–13 of the Student Book (the cover of *The Iron Man*). Without showing it to the group, the student must describe it so that the rest of the group can draw the illustration accurately on the A4 sheet. They can ask questions that will help them reconstruct the original, but must not look at it in the book. After five minutes, compare their version of the original and make any changes needed. Use a volunteer group to use their drawing as a prompt to describe the Iron Man to the rest of the class. They should use any words, phrases and similes remembered from the last lesson as well as their own words.

Development (20 minutes)

Choosing and using reading strategies to understand and retrieve simple information from fiction texts

Developing reader

Cycle A

Duration: 1 hour

Using Set B of the cut-up strips on a projector (resource sheet 2.1), display each in random order, reading each one aloud as you place it. Ask the students which words are unfamiliar, e.g. *brink* and *infrared*. Model how to use phonic knowledge to break a word into syllables and phonemes. Encourage students to explain the words by looking at the context in which they are used.

Give pairs of students a set of sentence strips. Ask them to take turns to read each sentence aloud and put them into an order that makes sense. Correct sequencing is not the main learning objective here: the activity is a device to get them to re-read whole sentences and to use phonic, grammar and context clues.

Take feedback, encouraging students to explain the clues they used to decide the order. Arrange the whiteboard strips in the correct order on the whiteboard and get the students to read them aloud. Then turn to the extract on page 12 of the Student Book and read it aloud yourself, with the students following to see where sentences begin and end. Ask them to say: how many sentences there are in the description (7) and how many times the following words are used: *iron/Iron* (5); *slowly* (2), *turned* (3). Encourage them to point to where these words are in the text.

Plenary (10 minutes)

Look at the sentence strips on a projector. Ask the students to find all the words that describe parts of the Iron Man's body. They can come to the board to underline them, then you can write them clearly in a list (*fingers, head, ears, eyes*). Ask them to underline and list verbs that end in -ing (*hearing, searching*). Ask them to underline and list verbs that end in -ed (*shaped, turned, glowed*).

Ask the students if they can see any other patterns or repetitions in the way language is used, e.g. *slowly turned to the right, slowly turned to the left … glowed white, then red, then infrared … turned this way … that way*. Suggest that these patterns make the story easier to remember. Switch off the projector and ask the students to think of the words they most remember from the text, then share them with a partner, or round the group.

Extension activity

Use look – say – cover – write – say – check to learn the nine words that have just been listed (*fingers, head, ears, eyes, hearing, searching, shaped, turned, glowed*).

Lesson Plan 1 of 3

Choosing and using reading strategies to understand and retrieve simple information from non-fiction texts

Developing reader

Cycle B

Duration: 1 hour

Resources needed	Lesson aims	Assessment Focuses
• CD-ROM Cycle B (Developing reader) resource sheet 1.1: starter activity quiz questions • Student Book pages 14–15: 'Monsters of the deep' photographs and fact cards • CD-ROM Cycle B (Developing reader) resource sheet 1.2: True/False questions based on fact cards • mini-whiteboards	• to know how to use phonic strategies to read unfamiliar words • to be able to use knowledge of grammar and context to read for meaning • to be able to recount the main facts in a non-fiction text **Target areas** • Target area 1: Choosing appropriate reading strategies • Target area 2: Scanning ahead to work out the structure of extended sentences • Target area 4: Reading for meaning to retrieve information from non-fiction texts	AF1, AF2, AF8

Starter (15 minutes)

Gather the students round the whiteboard. Display the following words and read them aloud in unison: *whale*, *squid*, *shark*, *octopus*, *plankton*, *krill*. Ask: 'Have you seen all these words before? Which ones, if any, are unfamiliar? What topic might include all these words? Can we suggest a title for the topic?' (e.g. large sea creatures). Highlight phonic patterns in the words that will help students to read and spell them independently, and practise segmenting and blending skills, using a game/quiz approach. Answers can be provided orally or written and shown on mini-whiteboards (see resource sheet 1.1 for questions).

Introduction (15 minutes)

Explain to the students that in the next few lessons they will be learning how to gather facts and information from non-fiction texts linked by the theme of huge sea creatures. Using pages 6–9 in the Student Book ('This is your brain' and 'How to be an active reader') if helpful, remind the students that reading is an active search for meaning, and should feel like brain gym! Three of the most helpful active reading strategies they can use to find information from texts are skimming, scanning and asking questions. Ask students to give themselves a traffic-light rating to show how confident they are about using each strategy (green = very confident, can do this easily; amber = quite confident but sometimes need help; red = not confident and need help with this). Tell them you will ask them to do this again when they have finished working on the lessons in this cycle.

Agree definitions of these three strategies, stressing what is active about them as processes, e.g. When we skim a text, we move our eyes quickly over it, from side to side and top to bottom, looking for the main ideas, using clues like pictures and headings. When we scan a text, we move our eyes a little more slowly across the text, searching for and picking out particular kinds of information such as names of people, places, numbers or dates. It's helpful to use a finger or a ruler to point out the information we're looking for so that we can pause on it, and look ahead and back to see where the sentence starts and ends. When we are looking for answers to questions, we need to move our eyes and pointers more slowly, looking for key words in the question and reading the whole sentence containing that word.

Development (20 minutes)

Practise these strategies as follows: ask students in pairs to turn to pages 14–15 in the Student Book, headed 'Monsters of the deep'. Give them 60 seconds to skim the pages, encouraging eye movements in zigzags across the page. Close the book. Students take turns, 20 seconds each, to tell their partner everything that they saw on the page. Open the book again.

Choosing and using reading strategies to understand and retrieve simple information from non-fiction texts

Developing reader

Cycle B

Duration: 1 hour

Individually, students scan the fact cards on pages 14–15 in the Student Book, looking for names of the sea creatures and numbers. Allow 60 seconds for this. Close the book. Ask: 'Which monsters of the deep are mentioned? Can you remember any of the numbers/measurements mentioned?'

Project the fact cards from resource sheet 1.2 (these will be used again in Lesson 2) and give out mini-whiteboards. Students write T (for True) on one side and F (for False) on the other. Read through each fact card, with the students following in the Student Book or on a projector. Ask the True/False questions one at a time, students holding up mini-whiteboards to display their answer. Help them to locate the correct information by highlighting the title of the relevant fact card and the bullet point that contains the answer. Confirm or correct their choices by reading out the whole of the relevant sentence and highlighting the key words that provided the answer.

Plenary (10 minutes)

Ask the students to rate how well they've used each strategy so far (skimming, scanning, asking questions) and to suggest other subject lessons where they can use these skills. With the fact cards displayed on a projector, divide the class into teams and get each team to make up and ask another True/False question. The answering team must come to the board to point to where they found the relevant information.

Extension activity

Practise skimming on: a newspaper front page, the back of a cereal packet, the cover of a fiction book.

Practise scanning for names of people in the main report on the front page of a newspaper; in the blurb on the back of a fiction book.

Lesson Plan
2 of 3

Choosing and using reading strategies to understand and retrieve simple information from non-fiction texts

Developing reader

Cycle B

Duration: 1 hour

Resources needed	Lesson aims	Assessment Focuses
• mini-whiteboards, pens and wipers • CD-ROM Cycle B (Developing reader) resource sheet 1.2: OHT of fact cards • CD-ROM Cycle B (Developing reader) resource sheet 2.1: 5W question cards and comprehension questions cut on OHT strips	• to know how to use phonic strategies to read unfamiliar words • to be able to use knowledge of grammar and context to read for meaning • to be able to recount the main facts in a non-fiction text • to be able to comment on obvious features of the text **Target areas** • Target area 1: Choosing appropriate reading strategies • Target area 2: Scanning ahead to work out the structure of extended sentences • Target area 4: Reading for meaning to retrieve information from non-fiction texts	AF1, AF2, AF8

Starter (15 minutes)

Display the following Latin names for two monsters of the deep: the great white shark = *Carcharadon carcharias* and the giant octopus = *Enteroctopus dofleini*. Issue a challenge: to be able to say both these Latin names and to spell one of them correctly within the next ten minutes. Ask: 'Is this impossible? What phonic knowledge can we use to help?' Show each Latin name on the board broken into syllables: Car/char/a/don car/char/i/as and En/ter/oc/to/pus do/flei/ni. Taking each word in turn, get students to clap, tap or stamp a rhythm as they say each syllable. Repeat several times, faster each time and finally from memory, e.g. with eyes closed, repeating after you. Look closely at the Latin name for the great white shark. Re-issue the challenge: to have a go at spelling this word from memory. Ask students to listen closely to the different sounds in the word as you say them syllable by syllable. Remind them of phonemes that they already know, e.g. *ch* and letter combinations they will recognise from other words, e.g. *don* as in *London*. Show them the syllables that are repeated in the two words. Highlight with them parts they think are tricky, e.g. the *i* in *ias* which sounds like an *e*. Get them to look closely at the two words for 20 seconds, saying them silently or aloud. Cover the Latin name and get students to have a go at writing it on mini-whiteboards as you say it. Hold up and show. Praise 'good guesses' and 'near misses'. Compare with original. Ask students to correct their version and show you again.

Introduction (15 minutes)

Remind students of the focus on skimming, scanning and asking questions in order to find facts and information in non-fiction texts. Explain that this lesson will concentrate on the strategy of asking questions and that this is a useful strategy because it makes us read a text more closely in order to find the right answer. Display the '5W and a How' questions on cut-up strips on a projector. Tell students that you are thinking of an object that is connected with the sea. They have to find out what your object is by asking you questions that start with one of the stems, e.g. 'Where is it usually found? What colour is it? Who might find it? How big is it?' etc. Get the students to ask questions and provide the answers for a few minutes, so that they can see how useful questions of this kind are (suitable objects to choose might be a shell, seaweed, a lighthouse.)

Explain that in the next part of the lesson they will be using information they have seen before, but will use the question stems to find out answers to more challenging questions.

Choosing and using reading strategies to understand and retrieve simple information from non-fiction texts

Developing reader

Cycle B

Duration: 1 hour

Development (20 minutes)
Display two of the fact cards from resource sheet 1.2 on a projector (giant squid and giant octopus) and read them with the students. Display the comprehension questions from resource sheet 2.1 one at a time. Model how to use the question stem to locate the right fact card and then the right place to look on the card, e.g: 'What does the giant squid look like? I need to look at the names on the fact cards and find the giant squid. Then I'm looking for details of *what* the squid looks like, so I need to pick out facts about its body shape and measurements, such as thick body, long tentacles, 15 metres long.' Highlight key words in the text that provide these answers. Repeat for the next two questions. Students work in pairs. Display the next set of questions about the giant octopus and ask students to find the answers. Provide correct answers to the questions and encourage students to explain *how* they located the relevant information.
Plenary (10 minutes)
Display the blue whale and great white shark fact cards and question stems. Divide the students into teams and get them to devise '5W and a How' questions to ask the opposing team. Students score points for providing the correct answer to a question and for explaining/showing where they found the information.
Extension activity
Find some long words that the students think will be as big a challenge to say and spell, as were the Latin names for the great white shark and the giant octopus. Ask each student to choose one to write down carefully and bring to the next lesson. They can add their words to a classroom display of challenging words.

Lesson Plan 3 of 3

Choosing and using reading strategies to understand and retrieve simple information from non-fiction texts

Developing reader

Cycle B

Duration: 1 hour

Resources needed	Lesson aims	Assessment Focuses
• Student Book pages 16–17: 'Sharks' text and summary of reading strategies • CD-ROM Cycle B (Developing reader) resource sheet 3.1: annotated shark text to model how to make notes	• to be able to recount the main facts in a non-fiction text • to be able to comment on obvious features of the text **Target areas** • Target area 1: Choosing appropriate reading strategies • Target area 2: Scanning ahead to work out the structure of extended sentences • Target area 4: Reading for meaning to retrieve information from non-fiction texts	AF1, AF2, AF5, AF6

Starter (15 minutes)

Display the following text (last paragraph of 'Sharks' text from Student Book page 17): 'A shark's teeth are triangular, and point backwards towards the throat. They have pointed tips and serrated edges, and cut just like a saw.' Ask students individually to read it to themselves, noting any words they have difficulty with. Then ask them to read it with a partner, taking a sentence each. Again, note any words they find difficult. Take feedback and display the difficult words. Work out together how to say them, using a range of strategies: phonic knowledge, grammar clues and context. Encourage students to read the whole sentence in which the word appears. Ask a volunteer to draw on the whiteboard what is being described, with help from the rest of the class. Label the drawing with key words and phrases from the description.

Introduction (15 minutes)

Explain to the students that what they have just read is one section from a longer text about sharks. They are going to read the whole text and use information from it to give a short talk about sharks to the class.

Turn to page 17 in the Student Book. Show students how to skim read the whole text by reading the first few words of the first sentence of each paragraph. Ask students to scan the text to find answers to the following questions: tell them they are scanning for names beginning with capital letters, and for a number: 'How many different kinds of sharks are there?' (more than 350). 'What are the names of two kinds of sharks?' (Pygmy Shark and Whale Shark). Ask them to find the fourth paragraph and then scan it to find the word *denticles*. Get them to read back from the word so that they can answer the question: 'What are denticles?'

Development (20 minutes)

Students work in pairs: give each pair a number from 1 to 5 and ask them to find the corresponding paragraph and to read it together. Ask for volunteer pairs to read aloud and hear the text read through in sequence. Remind them of their task: to use this information to give a short talk about sharks. Reorganise students into groups of three.

Using resource sheet 3.1 (OHT of text with note-making frame next to it), model how to make notes from the text that can be used to talk from. Encourage students to pick out and record key words from the text and to use visual symbols/quick drawings that will help them to sum up what the paragraph is about, as they did in the starter activity. Model this for the first and final paragraphs. Provide one copy of the text and notes frame for each group to complete.

Groups re-read the remaining paragraphs and complete the note-making frame. Practise speaking from the notes and rehearse the whole talk.

Lesson Plan
3 of 3

Choosing and using reading strategies to understand and retrieve simple information from non-fiction texts

Developing reader

Cycle B

Duration: 1 hour

Plenary (10 minutes)
Students give their talks to another group. Evaluate success by giving each other traffic-light ratings for the questions: 'Was the talk easy to follow and understand? Were all the main facts included?' Remind students of the strategies they have used in this cycle of lessons, using information on page 16 of the Student Book. Return to students' initial traffic-light ratings which showed how confident they were about using each of the reading strategies: skimming, scanning and asking questions (green = very confident, can do this easily; amber = quite confident but sometimes need help; red = not confident and need help with this). Ask them to update their ratings and explain them to a partner.
Extension activity
Give your talk about sharks to a friend or member of your family. Ask them for feedback about how well you did.

Using reading strategies independently to retrieve information from fiction texts

Developing reader

Cycle C

Duration: 1 hour

Resources needed	Lesson aims	Assessment Focuses
• CD-ROM Cycle C (Developing reader) resource sheet 1.1: phoneme cards for starter activity • Student Book pages 18–19: *Beowulf and Grendel* film poster(s) and questions • Student Book pages 20–21: stills from the film and reading strategy prompt questions	• to be able to extract information from simple fiction texts • to be able to comment on how information is presented in a text **Target areas** • Target area 2: Scanning ahead to work out the structure of extended sentences • Target area 3: Using active reading strategies • Target area 4: Reading for meaning to retrieve information from fiction texts	AF1, AF2, AF3, AF8

Starter (15 minutes)

The aim of the activity is to investigate medial vowels that make the *ee* phoneme. Begin with tongue-twisters that will introduce the medial vowel sounds made by the vowel phoneme *ee*, e.g: *The sea is as green as a bean; The heat beats hot on the street; The night steals away like a thief.* Write the following words on the whiteboard, saying them clearly and underlining the medial vowels that make the *ee* phoneme: *sea, green, bean, heat, beating, street, steals, thief.* Remind students that the same sound can be represented or spelt in more than one way. They are going to practise making words where the middle sound is represented by *ee, ea,* or *ie*. Using resource sheet 1.1, give a set of cut-up phoneme cards to pairs of students, or use a set cut from acetate for students to move around. Take each vowel phoneme card in turn and display it on a desk or projector. Students make as many words as they can by adding initial and final phonemes; they must make an actual word. Students should say the word aloud and can be challenged to explain its meaning, e.g. by using it in a sentence. All the words should have the same sound in the middle, e.g. *shield* but not *fried*. Examples: *feel, kneel, sheet, freed, cheat, peat, knead, bead, sheaf, thief, chief, shield.*

Introduction (15 minutes)

Using pages 18–19 of the Student Book, ask the students individually to look closely at the film poster for 60 seconds. Encourage them to skim for overall impression and to scan for detail, e.g. by running their eyes quickly across it in a zigzag movement, then imagining the poster divided into quarters and looking at each quarter for 10 seconds to remember what was in it. Tell them to close the book and tell a partner what they saw.

Remind students of how we find meaning when we read (page 8 of the Student Book), and as a class consider the questions next to the film poster, which are based on the different kinds of clues we use when reading independently. Answer some of the questions as a whole class, some in pairs and some individually. Encourage students to provide evidence and reasons for their answers.

Development (20 minutes)

Using the information on pages 20–21 of the Student Book, introduce the students to the story of Beowulf and Grendel. Look together at the film stills on page 21 of the Student Book and discuss answers to the questions which encourage students to use the reading strategies of visualising, questioning, predicting and speculating.

Make up short descriptions that could summarise what is happening in each of the stills and act as captions for them. Model one, then get students to work in pairs on the other, rehearsing orally before writing.

Plenary (10 minutes)

Pairs of students take turns to read out their descriptions. Take the two stills and together decide what

Using reading strategies independently to retrieve information from fiction texts

Developing reader

Cycle C

Duration: 1 hour

we would hear on the soundtrack of the film, e.g. type of music, sound effects and any dialogue.
Extension activity
Students decide which strategies they will use to learn how to spell the names of the main characters in the story: Grendel, Beowulf, Hrothgar.

Using reading strategies independently to retrieve information from fiction texts

Developing reader

Cycle C

Duration: 1 hour

Resources needed	Lesson aims	Assessment Focuses
• CD-ROM Cycle C (Developing reader) resource sheet 2.1: phonic strategies for spelling and reading • Student Book pages 20–21: storyboard from *Beowulf and Grendel* • CD-ROM Cycle C (Developing reader) resource sheet 2.2: cloze exercise on first paragraph of the *Beowulf and Grendel* story	• to be able to use punctuation cues when reading for meaning and read ahead in the text • to recognise when meaning does not make sense and be able to self-correct or problem-solve • to be able to extract information from simple fiction texts • to be able to comment on how information is presented in a text **Target areas** • Target area 2: Scanning ahead to work out the structure of extended sentences • Target area 3: Using active reading strategies • Target area 4: Reading for meaning to retrieve information from non-fiction texts	AF1, AF6, AF8

Starter (15 minutes)

Use resource sheet 2.1 to remind students of the phonic skills they have been using to help them read and spell accurately.

Using mini-whiteboards, use the following words for a spelling test. Say each word twice and give context clues; get students to write spelling choice. Ask: Does it look right? Does it sound right? Do you want to change anything? Encourage students to make changes without erasing the first version. Say the word again for a final check, then ask them to hold up whiteboards and show what they have written. Help each other to make any corrections needed by drawing attention to possible and best fit choices, e.g. 'Sam's spelt the ee phoneme in "sandy beach" with a double e; what other letters could he have used that make the same sound?'

Word list: *beach, branch, church, dance, danger, field, shield, fighting, fought.*

Introduction (15 minutes)

Turn to pages 20–21 in the Student Book and read again the outline of the *Beowulf and Grendel* story. Read the storyboard images. Encourage students to use visualising, questioning and predicting and speculating strategies to fill out details of what has happened before the events depicted in the storyboard and what might happen next.

Development (20 minutes)

Use the cloze resource sheet (2.2), projected onto a whiteboard and as a photocopy for students to complete. Model how to use context, grammar and punctuation clues to decide which word to place in the space. Give time for students to make choices in pairs, then provide feedback and correct answers by reading together the first paragraph of the story on OHT and/or page 22 of the Student Book. Read aloud with expression, modelling how to use punctuation clues to emphasise meaning.

Plenary (10 minutes)

Ask the students to explain what they found easy and what they found more difficult about the cloze exercise and what clues they used to help them make choices.

Get the students to retell events so far from the viewpoint of Beowulf.

Lesson Plan
2 of 3

Using reading strategies independently to retrieve information from fiction texts

Developing reader

Cycle C

Duration: 1 hour

Extension activity
Predict what will happen next in the story and say what clues you have used to decide.

Lesson Plan 3 of 3

Using reading strategies independently to retrieve information from fiction texts

Developing reader

Cycle C

Duration: 1 hour

Resources needed	Lesson aims	Assessment Focuses
• mini-whiteboards • CD-ROM Cycle C (Developing reader) resource sheet 3.1: sentence strips on card or OHT • Student Book page 20–23: the *Beowulf and Grendel* story	• to be able to use punctuation cues when reading for meaning and read ahead in the text • to recognise when meaning does not make sense and be able to self-correct or problem-solve • to be able to extract information from fiction texts • to be able to comment on how information is presented in a text **Target areas** • Target area 2: Scanning ahead to work out the structure of extended sentences • Target area 3: Using active reading strategies • Target area 4: Reading for meaning to retrieve information from non-fiction texts	AF5, AF6, AF8

Starter (15 minutes)

Remind students that some words can sound the same but be spelt differently. Draw a two-column grid on mini-whiteboards; label left column *word*; right column *meaning*. Play homophones, with the teacher providing either the correct spelling or the correct meaning and students completing the missing column.

Homophones word list: *hole, whole*; *reel, real*; *plain, plane*; *break, brake*; *fort, fought*; *stares, stairs*; *a loan, alone*.

Introduction (15 minutes)

Explain that to read for meaning accurately, students need to use punctuation clues, and knowledge about how sentences are constructed, and that this lesson will practise those skills.

Play a sentence-building game: write on the whiteboard the following simple sentence: *The man walked across the road*. Explain that this has one subject (*the man*) and one verb (*walked*). It makes complete sense and is called a main clause. Show how to change the sentence into one that could come from the *Beowulf and Grendel* story and could be made more interesting by:

- strengthening the nouns: Grendel **the monster** walked across the moor.
- strengthening the verb: Grendel the monster **stalked** across the moor.
- adding adjectives: The **bloodthirsty** monster, Grendel, stalked across the **misty, lonely** moor.
- adding a phrase that tells us more about time: **In the dead of night**, the bloodthirsty monster, Grendel, stalked across the misty, lonely moor.
- adding a subordinate clause (a group of words that includes a subject and verb but which doesn't make sense on its own until added to a main clause): **Hungry for blood and bones**, in the dead of night, the bloodthirsty monster, Grendel, stalked across the misty, lonely moor.

Get students to experiment with changing the order of the parts of the sentence around. Emphasise how punctuation is used to separate the different phrases and clauses in the sentence to help us to read it more clearly.

Lesson Plan 3 of 3

Using reading strategies independently to retrieve information from fiction texts

Developing reader

Cycle C

Duration: 1 hour

Development (20 minutes)
Explain that we need to know how complex sentences are constructed so that we can read ahead in the sentence to establish meaning and back in the sentence to check what we have read. Practising putting parts of sentences together and noticing the punctuation used will help us become more fluent readers. Use resource sheet 3.1 to manipulate sentences, adding subordinate clauses to main clauses and moving them around to see what the different effects are. Get the students to check the original version of the paragraph on page 22 of the Student Book. Read the rest of the story with the students, emphasising how meaning is created by adding details to main clauses. Highlight the punctuation effects. Get the students to re-read the story aloud with a partner, aiming to read with expression and a sense of drama.
Plenary (10 minutes)
Display the simple sentences below and experiment with different ways of combining them into one longer sentence. Notice what happens to the punctuation and encourage students to read aloud each time. Which version do they prefer? Grendel pushed the door. It gave way at once. He moved across the floor. He saw the warriors asleep. He reached out. He grabbed the nearest one. He bit into the flesh and bones.
Extension activity
Retell the whole story to a friend or someone at home. Choose whether to tell it in the third person or from the viewpoint of either Grendel or Beowulf.

Using reading strategies independently to retrieve information from non-fiction texts

Developing reader

Cycle D

Duration: 1 hour

Resources needed	Lesson aims	Framework Objectives
• CD-ROM Cycle D (Developing reader) resource sheet 1.1: starter activity: /k/ phoneme, printed as a set of cards, one per student, or as OHT cut-up strips • CD-ROM Cycle D (Developing reader) resource sheet 1.2: QUADS grid • Student Book pages 24–25: 'The Loch Ness Monster: fact or fiction?' Information about Loch Ness • CD-ROM Cycle D (Developing reader) resource sheet 1.3: copy of Loch Ness extract for text-marking	• to be able to use punctuation cues when reading for meaning and read ahead in the text • to recognise when meaning does not make sense and be able to self-correct or problem-solve • to be able to extract information from simple non-fiction texts **Target areas** • Target area 2: Scanning ahead to work out the structure of extended sentences • Target area 3: Using active reading strategies • Target area 4: Reading for meaning to retrieve information from non-fiction texts	Y7: R6, **R8** Y8: R4, **R5** **Assessment Focuses** AF2, AF3, AF4

Starter (15 minutes)

The aim of this activity is to explore the consonant phoneme /k/. Using the information on resource sheet 1.1 (as a handout for students' reference or on a projector) remind the students that the same sound (or phoneme) can be represented by different letters. Say or write the following words that contain the /k/ phoneme, asking students to choose the correct phoneme to complete the word. Students can do this by holding up the phoneme card or volunteers can place the correct choice on the projector. Provide a context clue for each word (examples below).

1 You'll need to wear your coat when you go out.

2 Have you got your football kit ready?

3 Lock the door when you go out.

4 Chris is cooking today.

5 In Scotland, a lake is called a loch.

Extend the activity by asking students to list as many words as they can where the initial /k/ phoneme is represented by the letter k (e.g. *kite*, *kitchen*, *keep*) and as many words as they can where the initial /k/ phoneme is represented by the letter *c* (e.g. *cake*, *call*, *crying*). Which is more common?

Challenge: use a dictionary to find words where the initial /k/ phoneme is spelt *ch* (e.g. *choir*, *chorus*, *chord*, *character*) Ask: 'How common is this spelling?'

Introduction (15 minutes)

Explain to students that in the next three lessons they will be using a range of reading strategies to find information about the Loch Ness Monster. They will collect and record information using a QUADS grid (question/answer/details/source). They will then decide their own answer to the question: 'Does the Loch Ness Monster exist?'

Brainstorm what the students already know about the Loch Ness Monster and display their ideas on a whiteboard or flipchart. Time this strictly and record ideas without comment. Highlight similar ideas and choose two or three to explore further. Ask: 'How do we know this? What evidence is there?' Stress that students will be gathering ideas about the Loch Ness Monster from different sources and that some of the information may support what they already think, while some of it may be completely new. They will need to record some of it so that they can think about the evidence and decide whether the Loch Ness Monster is fact or fiction.

Using reading strategies independently to retrieve information from non-fiction texts

Developing reader

Cycle D

Duration: 1 hour

Using the QUADS template on resource sheet 1.2 on OHT, model how to complete the first column. Explain that you want to find out more about Loch Ness to see if it's possible that a monster could live there. Decide suitable research questions and record on the grid: 'Where is Loch Ness and what is it like? Could a monster survive in it?'

Development (20 minutes)

Look together at the map and photograph showing Loch Ness on pages 24–25 of the Student Book . Gather initial responses to the question: 'Where is Loch Ness and what is it like?' Ask students to find the information entitled 'Facts about Loch Ness'. They should skim and scan the text individually, then compare their findings with a partner's.

Choose a sound or signal that students can use to signify a full stop, e.g. a hand clap or tap on the table. Read the first paragraph of the text aloud, asking students to signal when they 'hear' that a full stop is needed, i.e. because the sentence makes complete sense. Using resource sheet 1.3 'Facts about Loch Ness', model for students how to highlight the main subject words and verbs in each sentence, encouraging them to read ahead to the end of the sentence and back to its start to locate the main clause. Highlight pronouns that provide cohesion, e.g. *covered in ice* ... ***this ice***.

Students work in pairs to read aloud the second and third paragraphs to each other, again stressing where they hear the full stops and checking in the text. On a projector, work as a class to highlight the main clauses, as before.

In pairs, students decide answers to the questions about Loch Ness on the QUADS template in resource sheet 1.2.

Plenary (10 minutes)

Show the QUADS grid again and model how to record students' answers to the questions about Loch Ness in note form (see resource sheet 1.2 for an example of how this has been started). Encourage speculation in answer to whether a monster might live there, e.g. by asking if the loch is big enough; whether it might matter that the loch doesn't freeze; what the age of the loch might signify; any evidence to suggest that more than one monster has been seen, etc.

Extension activity

Ask three or four people if they think the Loch Ness Monster exists or not. Note down what they say to report back to the class.

Lesson Plan
2 of 3

Using reading strategies independently to retrieve information from non-fiction texts

Developing reader

Cycle D

Duration: 1 hour

Resources needed	Lesson aims	Assessment Focuses
• CD-ROM Cycle D (Developing reader) resource sheets 2.1 and 2.2: illustration and comprehension questions for starter activity • Student Book pages 26–27: photographs of the Loch Ness Monster • Student Book pages 28–29: eyewitness accounts of sightings	• to be able to use punctuation cues when reading for meaning and read ahead in the text • to be able to extract information from simple non-fiction texts • to recognise when meaning does not make sense and be able to self-correct or problem-solve • to be able to comment on how information is presented in a text **Target areas** • Target area 2: Scanning ahead to work out the structure of extended sentences • Target area 3: Using active reading strategies • Target area 4: Reading for meaning to retrieve information from non-fiction texts	AF2, AF3, AF4, AF6, AF8

Starter (15 minutes)

Gather the class round the whiteboard. Display the labelled drawing of a blue whale (resource sheet 2.1) and ask: 'Where might we find a text like this? What is it showing us?' Display and read the list of spelling strategies. Ask the students to scan the labelled drawing from top to bottom, then from left to right and identify any words that they have trouble reading straight away. Highlight these words and together apply the spelling strategies to them, drawing attention to key features and reminding students of familiar graphic and phonic patterns, e.g. the /k/ phoneme in *sickle-shaped* and *thick*; double consonants in *flipper* and *blubber*. Encourage them to use context clues provided by the drawing.

Cover the drawing and say the following words for students to spell, individually then checked in pairs or by a volunteer writing a word on the whiteboard for the class to agree or challenge: *flukes, sickle-shaped, baleen, throat, grooves, flippers, blubber.*

Uncover the drawing and get students to locate words and check spellings.

Introduction (15 minutes)

Ask: 'What does the Loch Ness Monster look like?' Hear ideas from the class. Direct the students to pages 26–27 of the Student Book and the selection of 'photographs' of the monster.

Individually, ask students to draw one animal based on all the information shown in the pictures.

In small groups, students compare their drawings and highlight similarities and differences in them.

Development (20 minutes)

Show the eyewitness descriptions of the Loch Ness Monster on resource sheet 2.2. The students' task is to match each description to the right eyewitness. Direct them to pages 28–29 in Student Book: the eyewitness accounts of sightings of the Loch Ness Monster. Model for students how to scan for speech marks in the accounts that provide descriptions of the monster, which will enable them to match the information more quickly. Students can work individually or in pairs on this activity; check answers as a whole class.

Answers: Description A = Hugh Ayton; B = 3 the Spicers; C = 5 Torquil McCleod; D = 6 Alex

Using reading strategies independently to retrieve information from non-fiction texts

Developing reader

Cycle D

Duration: 1 hour

Campbell; E = 7 John McLeod; F = 8 the Boyds; G = 9 Mrs Mackay.
Plenary (10 minutes)
Show the QUADS grid used in Lesson 1 (resource sheet 1.2). As a class, enter details in answer to the question: What does the Loch Ness Monster look like?
Extension activity
Does the Loch Ness Monster exist? On the evidence you've read so far, how would you answer this question?

Lesson Plan
3 of 3

Using reading strategies independently to retrieve information from non-fiction texts

Developing reader

Cycle D

Duration: 1 hour

Resources needed	Lesson aims	Assessment Focuses
• CD-ROM Cycle D (Developing reader) resource sheet 3.1: picture of plesiosaur • Student Book pages 28–29: eyewitness accounts of sightings • CD-ROM Cycle D (Developing reader) resource sheet 1.2: QUADS grid	• to be able to use punctuation cues when reading for meaning and read ahead in the text • to recognise when meaning does not make sense and be able to self-correct or problem-solve • to be able to extract information from simple non-fiction texts **Target areas** • Target area 2: Scanning ahead to work out the structure of extended sentences • Target area 3: Using active reading strategies • Target area 4: Reading for meaning to retrieve information from non-fiction texts	AF2, AF3, AF4, AF6

Starter (15 minutes)

Using resource sheet 3.1, show the picture of a plesiosaur and read the details with students. Give them 2 minutes to practise individually describing the features of a plesiosaur, using information from the drawing. Model the start of this for them if needed, e.g. 'It has a long, thin curved neck which has spiky scales along the top surface and underneath …' You could also support the activity by asking questions about the creature based on the drawings, e.g. 'How do you think the creature moves through the water?'

In pairs, students take it in turns to role-play a conversation between an eyewitness who has just seen what they think is a plesiosaur in Loch Ness, and a journalist asking them questions about it.

Introduction (15 minutes)

Remind students of their task: by the end of the lesson they will have completed the QUADS grid and will use it to explain their conclusion about whether or not the Loch Ness Monster exists.

Return to the eyewitness accounts on pages 28–29 of the Student Book. Ask the students to sort the accounts into a timeline, reminding them to scan the accounts by looking for dates. Students individually should write the numbers of the accounts in order of dates of sightings, then agree in pairs or threes. You can agree the order as a whole class by getting the class to arrange volunteers into an agreed 'washing line' of date order, moving students into position and checking the information in the text as they do this.

Answers: date 1 = eyewitness 1; date 2 = eyewitness 7; date 3 = eyewitness 9; date 4 = eyewitness 3; date 5 = eyewitness 4; date 6 = eyewitness 6; date 7 = eyewitness 5; date 8 = eyewitness 2; date 9 = eyewitness 8.

Development (20 minutes)

Students work individually to re-read the eyewitness accounts and to decide which accounts they find most and least convincing. They should choose three or four of the accounts they think are the most important in helping to decide if the Loch Ness Monster exists or not, and place them in priority order, with 1 being the most important.

As a whole class, decide which details to record on the QUADS grid (resource sheet 1.2) in answer to the questions: 'Who says they have seen the Loch Ness Monster? Who do you most believe and why?'

Using reading strategies independently to retrieve information from non-fiction texts

Developing reader

Cycle D

Duration: 1 hour

Plenary (10 minutes)
Gather responses to the last question on the QUADS grid: 'Why is it hard to say for certain if the Loch Ness Monster exists?' Give a few minutes for students individually to consider the evidence on the completed grid. Take a class vote in answer to the question: 'Does the Loch Ness Monster exist?' Count the number who vote Yes, No or Not sure.
Extension activity
Write your own answer to the question: Does the Loch Ness Monster exist?

Using reading strategies independently to retrieve information from texts

Developing reader

Assessment

Duration: 1 hour

Resources needed	Lesson aims	Assessment Focuses
• Teacher's Guide page 27: starter activity: illustration of comparative sizes of different creatures; comprehension questions • Teachers Guide page 28: spelling strategies for unfamiliar words • Teacher's Guide page 29: list of reading strategies (reproduced as photocopy for student's reference or set of cards) • Teacher's Guide page 30: OHT strips or card for modelling how to work out the structure of extended sentences • Student Book pages 30–31: 'Who has seen the Loch Ness Monster?'	• to be able to use punctuation cues when reading for meaning and read ahead in the text • to be able to extract information from simple non-fiction texts • to be able to comment on how information is presented in a text **Target areas** • Target area 2: Skimming and scanning • Target area 3: Understanding text layout and organisation • Target area 4: Reading for meaning to retrieve information from non-fiction texts	AF1, AF2, AF3, AF4, AF5, AF6

Starter (15 minutes)

Display the illustration showing the relative sizes of blue whales and dinosaurs. Ask: 'What information are we given here? Where might we find this kind of information?' Encourage students to use the spelling strategies to help them say the names aloud. Answer the comprehension questions together, using this exercise to reinforce students' understanding of how to read this kind of information and of the concept of scale. Encourage students to pronounce the names clearly when they answer the questions. Encourage them to explain how they arrived at the answer.

For an additional challenge, get students to nominate the hardest name to spell. Can they use the listed strategies to learn the spelling?

Answers to comprehension questions (rounded to nearest figure):

1 Compsognathus is the smallest; blue whale is the largest.

2 24–31 metres.

3 8–10.

4 About the same.

5 40–50.

Introduction (15 minutes)

Display the learning objective for the next three lessons: to be able to using reading strategies independently to retrieve information from fiction and non-fiction texts. Explain to students that in this lesson they will be working as a whole class on a short text, to gain confidence in using reading strategies to retrieve information, before working more independently in the following two lessons. The topic of the texts will be familiar, as they are connected by the theme of fictional or real-life monsters.

Using page 29 of the Teacher's Guide, introduce the reading strategies that students will be using in the Assessment Task. Check students' understanding of them by asking them to explain how they have used any of these strategies in recent lessons. If the resource is cut up onto separate cards, you can ask students to sort them in various ways and discuss findings, e.g. arranged in order of usefulness; arranged according to how confident students are in using them; arranged in sequence of

Lesson Plan
1 of 3

Using reading strategies independently to retrieve information from texts

Developing reader

Assessment

Duration: 1 hour

use when approaching an unfamiliar text, etc. You can ask students to rate themselves on how independently they think they can use each strategy to retrieve information from a new text and use results to sort peer pairs/small groups to work together during the next two lessons.

Development (20 minutes)

Direct students to page 30–31 of the Student Book: an eyewitness account of the Loch Ness Monster. Show students how to skim-read the text by reading just the first part of the first sentence and the last part of the last sentence in each paragraph. Ask them to say what the text is about and what type of text it is, i.e. first-person recount. Ask students in pairs to scan the text for the following answers to 'W' questions: **Who** saw the Loch Ness monster? Scan for names with capital letters and words denoting family members. **When** did they see it? Scan for dates and times of day. **Where** did they see it? Scan for place names. **What** did it look like? Use the drawing to describe its appearance. (There is no need to read the whole text at this point, as students will be doing this independently in the next lesson.)

Point out to students that the text contains some very long sentences and that they will need to use punctuation and grammar clues to help them read these confidently and with understanding. Using the resource on page 30 of the Teacher's Guide, model how to separate and reconstruct the different phrases and clauses in the first example, highlighting the main clause and the use of punctuation to emphasise the different parts of the sentence. Working in pairs or threes, get students to do the same on the next example, encouraging them to find the main clause and then experiment with the order in which clauses and phrases can be rearranged. This can be done by cutting the sentences into strips to be rearranged or by students using mini-whiteboards to write down the extended sentence.

Plenary (10 minutes)

Hear/see students' reconstructed sentences. Emphasise the work done by the punctuation, e.g. use of commas to separate phrases, subordinate clauses or items in a list; full stop to mark the end of a completed clause. Ask students to locate the extended sentences in the whole text and to read a little way back and ahead to establish context. They can then find further examples of extended sentences in the text, e.g. by locating the full stop and reading back to see where the sentence starts.

Extension activity

Reflect on the use of reading strategies in this lesson. Which of those listed have you used? How did you use them? How did they help you?

Developing reader

Starter activity

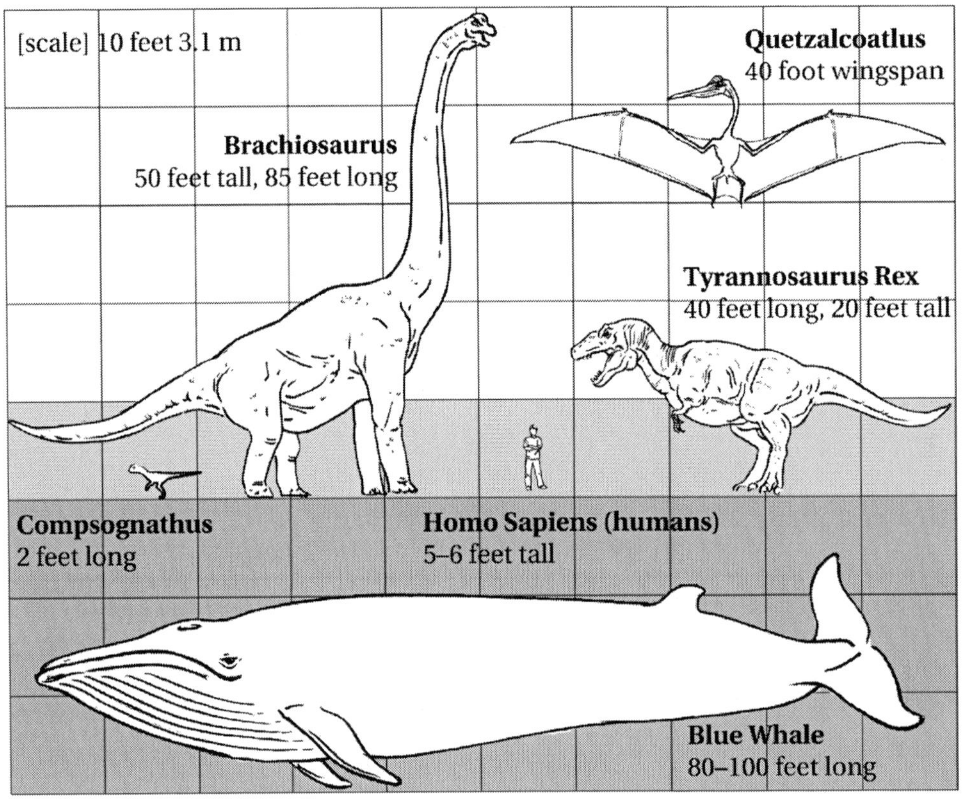

Scale: 1 square = 3.1 metres

Spelling strategies for unfamiliar words

Can I sound the word out?

Can I work out the word from the initial sound?

Can I recognise any features within the word that I can read?

Does it sound right?

Does it make sense in context?

Comprehension questions

1 Which is the smallest creature and which is the tallest?

2 How many metres long is the blue whale?

3 How many humans would make up the height of a Brachiosaurus?

4 Is the wingspan of a Quetzalcoatlus shorter, longer or about the same as the length of a Tyrannosaurus Rex?

5 How many Compsognathus would equal the length of a blue whale?

Developing reader

Reading strategies: things we do as we read that help us make sense of a text

• **using prior knowledge:** What I already know about the topic	• **checking vocabulary:** Does that word make sense? Have I read it correctly? Does it fit with what I've read so far?
• **re-reading:** Looking back in the text when I don't understand	• **asking questions:** To help me understand the text and find information I need
• **predicting and speculating:** Using clues to work out what might come next	• **visualising:** Picturing what is happening
• **skimming:** To get an idea what the text is about	• **scanning:** To find specific information in the text

Developing reader

The Loch Ness Monster

Rearrange the parts of this extended sentence in different ways, adding the correct punctuation.

Example for teacher modelling

on the return journey	,	
at a place where the road runs very close to the Loch	,	
about three miles from Foyers	,	
my sister suddenly shouted	,	"
look there's the monster	"	.

On the return journey, at a place where the road runs very close to the Loch, about three miles from Foyers, my sister suddenly shouted, "Look, there's the Monster".

Example for students to try

we watched in awe and amazement	,
for over 5 minutes	,
then it suddenly swung round away from the shore	,
and shot across the Loch at a terrific speed	,
putting up a wash	.

We watched in awe and amazement, for over 5 minutes, then it suddenly swung round away from the shore, and shot across the Loch at a terrific speed, putting up a wash.

Lesson Plan 2 of 3

Using reading strategies independently to retrieve information from texts

Developing reader

Assessment

Duration: 1 hour

Resources needed	Lesson aims	Assessment Focuses
• Student Book pages 30–31: Mrs Moir's account of sighting the Loch Ness Monster • Teacher's Guide page 32: reading assessment based on Mrs Moir's account • Teacher's Guide page 33: copies of the mark scheme for the assessment either on OHT or one per pair	• to be able to use punctuation cues when reading for meaning and read ahead in the text • to recognise when meaning does not make sense and be able to self correct or problem solve • to be able to extract information from simple non-fiction texts • to be able to comment on how information is presented in a text **Target areas** • Target area 2: Skimming and scanning • Target area 3: Understanding text layout and organisation • Target area 4: reading for meaning to retrieve information from non-fiction texts	AF2, AF3, AF4, AF6

Starter (15 minutes)

Recap on reading strategies that students will use to help them complete two short Assessment Tasks, one during this lesson and one in the next lesson. Direct them to Mrs Moir's account on pages 30–31 of the Student Book and the reading assessment on page 32 of the Teacher's Guide. Read the questions with students and clarify understanding; show them how to highlight key words and instructions in the question, e.g. 'In the third paragraph'; 'Include four details.'

Introduction (15 minutes)

Students in pairs/small groups read the whole text, using the strategies they know for dealing with unfamiliar words. The teacher can work with a guided group of weaker students in order to see how well they can tackle a text independently and to cue them in to strategies that will help them.

As a whole class, explain any words/phrases that students are still struggling with and highlight strategies used for decoding.

Development (20 minutes)

Individually, students complete the Assessment Task questions.

Plenary (10 minutes)

Using the mark scheme on page 33 of the Teacher's Guide, get students in pairs to assess each other's answers.

Extension activity

Reflect on the use of reading strategies in this lesson. Which of those listed have you used? How did you use them? How did they help you?

Developing reader

Assessment Task 1
Seeing the Loch Ness Monster

Name ______________________ Date ____________

1. How many people saw the Loch Ness Monster on the October afternoon in 1936? Who shouted, 'Look there's the Monster'?

____

____

(2 marks)

2. Why didn't they take a photograph of the monster?

____

____

(1 mark)

3. Read again the **third** paragraph that starts: 'There were three humps …' Label the drawing below with the details of what Mrs Moir saw. Include **four** different details.

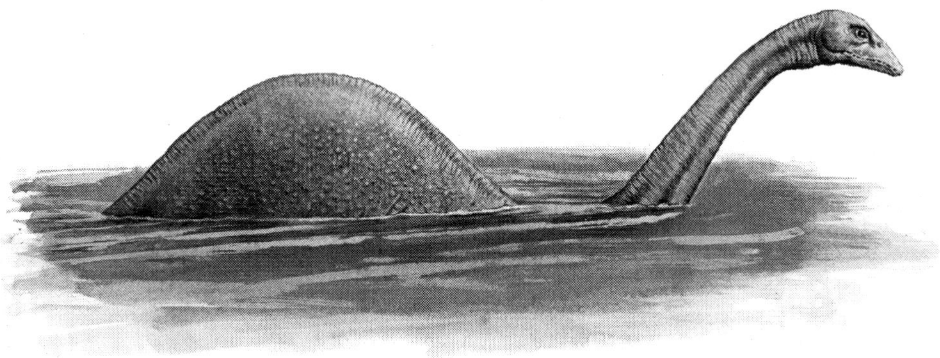

(4 marks)

4. In the **second** paragraph, Mrs Moir calls the Loch Ness Monster a 'wonderful creature'. List **two more** words or phrases from her account that show how much she admires the monster.

____

____

(2 marks)

5. At the end of her account, Mrs Moir says: 'A thrilling experience – I actually saw the Loch Ness monster.' List any **three** details from the text that most make you believe her story.

____

____

____

(6 marks)

Developing reader

Assessment mark scheme: Seeing the Loch Ness Monster

1. How many people saw the Loch Ness Monster on the October afternoon in 1936? Who shouted, 'Look there's the Monster'? (AF2; 2 marks)

   Five people saw the Monster (Mrs Moir, her sister, her mother-in-law, her daughter, her friend) 1 mark
   Her sister shouted, 'Look, there's the monster.' 1 mark

2. Why didn't they take a photograph of the monster? (AF3; 2 marks)

   They didn't have a camera with them ('alas! we had neither camera nor binoculars') 1 mark

3. Read again the **third** paragraph that starts: 'There were three humps …' Label the drawing below with the details of what Mrs Moir saw. Include **four** different details. (AF2; 4 marks)

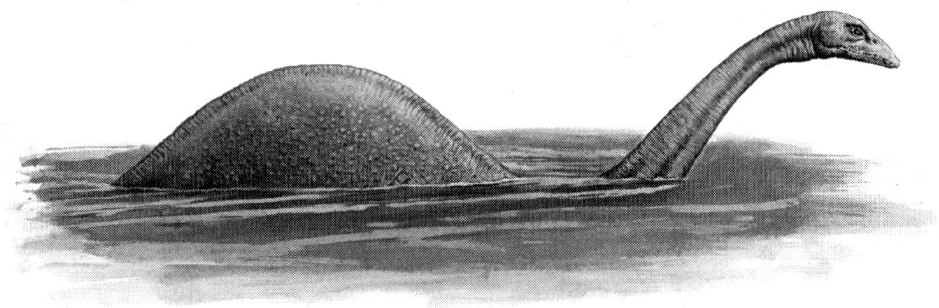

(4 marks)

4. In the **second** paragraph, Mrs Moir calls the Loch Ness Monster a 'wonderful creature'. List **two more** words or phrases from her account that show how much she admires the monster. (AF2; 2 marks)

   1 mark each for any of:
   - long *slender* neck
   - graceful/gracefully
   - we watched in awe and amazement
   - a huge creature, very powerful
   - quite at ease in the water
   - a thrilling experience

5. At the end of her account, Mrs Moir says: 'A thrilling experience – I actually saw the Loch Ness monster.' List any **three** details from the text that most make you believe her story.

   Several choices possible, up to 2 marks for each different one according to how relevant and well explained, e.g. including quotation or reference to the text:
   - five different people saw it
   - they watched it for a long time – 5 minutes, then 15 minutes
   - they got up close to the monster and could see it clearly
   - Mrs Moir describes it in a lot of detail/mentions several different features
   - she says that she actually saw it
   - she made a detailed drawing of it (AF3; 6 marks)

Using reading strategies independently to retrieve information from texts

Developing reader

Assessment

Duration: 1 hour

Resources needed	Lesson aims	Assessment Focuses
• Student Book pages 32–33: illustration and text about Minotaur • Teacher's Guide page 35: Assessment criteria for the task • Teacher's Guide pages 36–41: Assessment Task 3: individual copies of text and questions/instructions • highlighter pens for text-marking	• to be able to use a range of reading strategies independently • to be able to extract information from simple non-fiction texts **Target areas** • Target area 3: Using active reading strategies • Target area 4: Reading for meaning to retrieve information from texts	AF1, AF2, AF3

Starter (15 minutes)

Using the grid on page 35 of the Teacher's Guide, either enlarged and projected onto the whiteboard or as individual copies for students, introduce students to the two Assessment Focuses (AFs) for reading that describe the skills they have been working on for the last few lessons, matched to National Curriculum Level descriptors. Explain that in this lesson they will be working independently on a short Assessment Task and will be assessed using these criteria.

Direct students to pages 32–33 of the Student Book, illustration of the Minotaur and the story of Theseus' defeat of the Minotaur. Explain meaning of 'minotaur' i.e. *taurus* = Greek word for bull; *Minos* = King of Crete; hence: 'Minos's bull'. Students in pairs look at the illustration of the Minotaur and describe to each other what they see. Based on this information, why do they think it would be hard for Theseus to defeat the Minotaur? Take brief feedback.

Introduction (15 minutes)

Give out individual copies of the Assessment Task (Teacher's Guide pages 36–37). Read through the Assessment Task with students and clarify understanding of what they have to do. They will answer most questions by highlighting the text itself so will need their own copy (see Teacher's Guide page 38).

Students work independently to complete the Assessment Task. The teacher can work with a guided group of weaker students to observe and assist in completion of the task, or work with individuals, e.g. to listen to them read the extract whilst taking a running record (see introduction to Teacher's Guide page xiii).

Development (20 minutes)

Students work independently to complete the Assessment Task.

Plenary (10 minutes)

Complete self-assessment star rating using the criteria in the 'Assess your progress' box on page 33 of Student Book or page 41 in the Teacher's Guide.

Some answers can be marked by students, using the resource on pages 39–40 of the Teacher's Guide.

Extension activity

Look for the story of Theseus and the Minotaur in a library or on the Internet. Does it have a different ending to the one you read during the lesson?

Developing reader

Assessment criteria for task

Name ______________________ Date ____________

Assessment Focuses for Reading	If I'm Level 2 I can ...	If I'm Level 3 I can ...
AF2 Understand, describe, select or retrieve information, events and ideas from texts and use quotation and reference to text	• use different strategies to read unfamiliar words, e.g. phonic knowledge, grammar and context clues. • scan text to locate specific details. • identify and select the main ideas in texts. • usually notice when something I read doesn't make sense and go back and correct it. • read ahead to make sense of the whole sentence.	• use a range of reading strategies independently to tackle unfamiliar words. • identify straightforward and more obvious points in texts although I sometimes misunderstand. • quote from, or refer to, the text to back up my points, although I don't always choose relevant evidence.
AF3 Deduce, infer or interpret information, events or ideas from texts	• understand straightforward facts and ideas in texts. • recount main events or facts with some help. • express an opinion or preference. • find some details in the text in answer to specific questions.	• understand factual information and literal meanings in texts. • try to read between the lines to find deeper meanings. • make straightforward comments when talking about a text. • give a personal view about a text. • try to quote some details from the text or refer to information in it that supports my ideas..

Developing reader

Assessment Task: Theseus and the Minotaur

Name ______________________________ Date ______________

Before you read the whole text:

- Scan the text to find all the names that have a capital letter. Highlight these words in one colour.
- Skim the text to get an idea of what the story is about. Do this by reading the first sentence in each paragraph and the very last sentence of the story. Now read the statements below and circle the correct answer:

King Minos ruled the people of Crete.	True	False	Don't know
Theseus was the Prince of Crete.	True	False	Don't know
The Minotaur was kept in a labyrinth.	True	False	Don't know
Ariadne put a sword into Theseus' hand.	True	False	Don't know
The labyrinth was brightly lit.	True	False	Don't know
Theseus failed to kill the Minotaur.	True	False	Don't know

As you read the whole text:

- Underline the words in the text that you weren't able to recognise and read straight away.
- Use the strategies you know to make sense of an unfamiliar word:
  - o sound it out
  - o look for patterns you know
  - o think what word would fit in the sentence
- use context clues to help decide what the word could be.
- Now circle any words you still can't read.

Developing reader

After you've read the whole text:

- The following sentences have been wrongly copied from the story. Find each sentence in the text and correct the wrong version by highlighting the mistakes and writing the correct word above it.

  At the very centre of this tunnel, he kept a terrible monster, the Minotaur, who was always angry for human flesh.

  Ariadne, King Minos' son, was deeply ashamed of his father's cruelty and wanted to end it.

  Suddenly, the Minotaur came rushing towards him, screaming loudly.

- Put the events in the story into the right order. Number them 1–5 to show the order in which they happened.

  Ariadne gave Theseus a ball of string so he could find his way out of the labyrinth.

  King Minos of Crete built a labyrinth and kept the Minotaur inside it.

  Theseus fought the Minotaur and killed it.

  One year, Theseus went to Crete to fight the Minotaur.

  Every year, King Minos told his neighbours they must send him fourteen young men and women to feed the Minotaur.

- Answer these questions about the text by putting a tick next to the answer you think is right:

  1 Where was the labyrinth?

  a In the garden of King Minos' palace
  b In Athens
  c In a cellar underneath King Minos' palace

  2 Why did King Minos build the labyrinth and keep the Minotaur inside it?

  a to make Theseus angry
  b to amuse himself
  c because he was mad

  3 Which word best describes King Minos?

  a powerful
  b rich
  c cruel

  4 Why did Ariadne give Theseus a ball of string?

  a so he could tie the Minotaur's legs together
  b so they could each hold one end of it
  c so he could it rewind it and find his way back out of the labyrinth

  5 Which word best describes Theseus?

  a silly
  b brave
  c cruel

Developing reader

A long time ago on the island of Crete, King Minos ruled his people through force and fear. To amuse himself, he built a palace with a deep cellar beneath it, full of twisting tunnels and dead ends. At the very centre of this labyrinth he kept a terrible monster, the Minotaur, who was always hungry for human flesh. Every year King Minos threatened his neighbours, 'Unless you send me seven juicy young men and seven young and tender women to feed my beast, I'll sink your ships and make war on you.'

One year, Prince Theseus of Athens said to his father, King Aegeus, 'This madness has to stop. This year I'll go as one of the fourteen chosen ones and I will kill the Minotaur!' And nothing the king could say would change his mind.

At the entrance to the labyrinth, Theseus felt his bravery draining away. Deep in the darkness he heard the Minotaur, half man, half bull, stamping and snorting, its hoofs and horns scraping the walls of the maze.

Then Theseus felt a ball of string pushed into his hand. Ariadne, King Minos' daughter, was deeply ashamed of her father's cruelty and determined to end it. Now she whispered, 'Here, Theseus, take this. Tie one end around this stone pillar and unwind the string as you go. Then you can find your way back out of the labyrinth.'

Theseus inched forward into the darkness. Suddenly the Minotaur was crashing towards him, bellowing loudly. One bony horn caught Theseus's arm and gashed it open but Theseus fought back strongly. He darted around the monster, flicking the loose end of the string into its face, and diving out of sight beneath its belly, until he had sent the beast half mad with frustration. Once the Minotaur was distracted, Theseus leapt onto its back and grabbed one of its horns, forcing the creature's head backwards. He drew back his arm and plunged his dagger hard into the Minotaur's neck. The great beast shuddered and roared with pain, then slowly sank to the cold stone floor, defeated.

Developing reader

Assessment Task: Theseus and the Minotaur answers

These questions are testing students' ability to skim and scan independently and to retrieve simple facts from the text

Before you read the whole text:

- Scan the text to find all the names that have a capital letter. Highlight these words in one colour.
- Skim the text to get an idea of what the story is about. Do this by reading the first sentence in each paragraph and the very last sentence of the story. Now read the statements below and circle the correct answer:

King Minos ruled the people of Crete.	<u>True</u>	False	Don't know
Theseus was the Prince of Crete.	True	<u>False</u>	Don't know
The Minotaur was kept in a labyrinth.	<u>True</u>	False	Don't know
Ariadne put a sword into Theseus' hand.	True	<u>False</u>	Don't know
The labyrinth was brightly lit.	True	<u>False</u>	Don't know
Theseus failed to kill the Minotaur.	True	<u>False</u>	Don't know

Count 'Don't know' answers as being incorrect

These questions are testing students' ability to use a range of strategies (phonic and grammatical knowledge, context clues) to make sense of unfamiliar words, and their ability to self-correct when meaning doesn't make sense.

As you read the whole text:

- Underline the words in the text that you weren't able to recognise and read straight away.
- Use the strategies you know to make sense of an unfamiliar word:
  - sound it out
  - look for patterns you know
  - think what word would fit in the sentence
- use context clues to help decide what the word could be.
- Now circle any words you still can't read.

Developing reader

These questions are testing students' ability to identify and select main ideas, read ahead to make sense of the whole sentence, understand straightforward facts and ideas in texts and recount main events.

After you've read the whole text:

- The following sentences have been wrongly copied from the story. Find each sentence in the text and correct the wrong version by highlighting the mistakes and writing the correct word above it.

  labyrinth
  At the very centre of this tunnel, he kept a terrible monster, the Minotaur, who was
  hungry
  always angry for human flesh.

  daughter her
  Ariadne, King Minos' son, was deeply ashamed of his father's cruelty and wanted to end it.

  crashing bcllowing
  Suddenly, the Minotaur came rushing towards him, screaming loudly.

- Put the events in the story into the right order. Number them 1–5 to show the order in which they happened.

Ariadne gave Theseus a ball of string so he could find his way out of the labyrinth.	**4**
King Minos of Crete built a labyrinth and kept the Minotaur inside it.	**1**
Theseus fought the Minotaur and killed it.	**5**
One year, Theseus went to Crete to fight the Minotaur.	**3**
Every year, King Minos told his neighbours they must send him fourteen young men and women to feed the Minotaur.	**2**

- Answer these questions about the text by putting a tick next to the answer you think is right:

1 Where was the labyrinth?

c In a cellar underneath King Minos' palace

2 Why did King Minos build the labyrinth and keep the Minotaur inside it?

b to amuse himself

3 Which word best describes King Minos?

c cruel

4 Why did Ariadne give Theseus a ball of string?

c so he could it rewind it and find his way back out of the labyrinth

5 Which word best describes Theseus?

b brave

Developing reader

Assessment Task: Theseus and the Minotaur

Name ______________________________ Date ______________

You have been learning:

- to use reading strategies independently to understand and retrieve information from texts.

Give yourself a 1–3 star rating for each of the skills listed below. 3 stars = I can do this easily; 2 stars = I can do this with some help; 1 star = I need a lot of help with this.

Your teacher will also assess you ✓ = you can do this independently; ? = you need some help with this; X = you still need a lot of help with this.

Assessment criteria	Your assessment rating	Teacher assessment
• use different strategies to read unfamiliar words, e.g. phonic knowledge, grammar and context clues.		
• scan text to locate specific details.		
• identify and select the main ideas in texts.		
• usually notice when something I read doesn't make sense and go back and correct it.		
• read ahead to make sense of the whole sentence.		
• understand straightforward facts and ideas in texts.		
• recount main events or facts with some help.		
• express an opinion or preference.		
• find some details in the text in answer to specific questions.		

Lesson Plan 1 of 3

Reading for meaning in fiction texts, supporting ideas with evidence from the text

Secure developing reader

Cycle A

Duration: 1 hour

Resources needed	Lesson aims	Assessment Focuses
• CD-ROM Cycle A (Secure developing reader) resource sheet 1.1: starter activity: ar sound chart, one copy per pair; consonant cards to use with ar sound chart, one copy per pair, cut into cards • Student Book pages 34–35: film images; taglines and plotlines	• to be able to read simple unfamiliar texts accurately • to know how to scan a text to locate relevant information and read ahead independently **Target areas** • Target area 1: Finding and using textual reference • Target area 2: Skimming and scanning • Target area 3: Understanding text layout and organisation	AF2, AF3, AF4, AF6

Starter (15 minutes)

Show the students all the different letter combinations that make the *ar* sound: *a* in *fast, mast, last* etc. (but note regional variations where *a* is pronounced short); *al* in *calm* and *palm*; *ar* in *star, chart, art, jar*; *ear* in only one word: *heart.*

Give a copy of the phoneme chart (resource sheet 1.1) to students in pairs (or get them to make a copy on mini-whiteboards). Give a set of consonant cards per pair (or display on OHT and get students to write their choices on whiteboards.) Time students to see how many different words they can make containing the *ar* sound by adding consonant phonemes in different positions. Get them to say the words as they decide them and check for the correct sound.

Discuss with students the usual position of the *ar* sound: most often in the middle or at the end of the word.

Introduction (15 minutes)

Explain that in the next five cycles of lessons, students will be exploring ideas and texts connected by the theme of space exploration and imaginary or 'alien' worlds beyond the Earth. Give out plain cards and ask students to draw and label the way they imagine life on other planets. Collect in these cards and then give them out at random to pairs of students. Ask pairs to discuss the images of life in space that are described and to say whether or not they agree with these views. Pass on three or four different responses. As a whole class, using an interactive whiteboard or flipchart, pool students' ideas about life beyond our own planet in the form of a concept map ('Alien worlds' at the centre) which can be added to in subsequent lessons.

Development (20 minutes)

Direct the students to pages 34–35 of the Student Book: images from films about 'alien worlds'. Remind them what readers do when they skim a text to get an overall impression of it and when they scan a text to look for specific information.

Encourage students to skim the images in order to decide:

- What kind of texts are these? (film posters and stills)
- What is their purpose? (to advertise the film; to encourage people to go and see it)
- Where would you find them? (at cinemas, in film magazines, on film websites)

Explain the term 'plot outline' (a summary of the story). In pairs, ask students to scan the images and the plot outlines in order to decide:

- Which films feature wars or battles?
- Which films feature alien creatures from other planets?

Reading for meaning in fiction texts, supporting ideas with evidence from the text

Secure developing reader

Cycle A

Duration: 1 hour

- What special powers do people/creatures in these films have?
- Which alien world or creature sounds the most threatening to humans?
- Which alien world or creature sounds the least threatening to humans?

Working in pairs or small groups, students match the correct film image to the correct plot outline.

Take feedback and encourage students to explain the clues they used in making the match.

Plenary (10 minutes)

Discuss with students other films and books they know that are about worlds beyond the Earth. Why do they think people are so interested in this topic?

Add a summary of their comments to the 'Alien Worlds' concept map.

Extension activity

Ask a range of people about their favourite science-fiction book or film. Which part of it (or quotes from it) do they most remember?

Lesson Plan 2 of 3

Reading for meaning in fiction texts, supporting ideas with evidence from the text

Secure developing reader

Cycle A

Duration: 1 hour

Resources needed	Lesson aims	Assessment Focuses
• CD-ROM Cycle A (Secure developing reader) resource sheets 2.1, 2.2 and 2.3: starter activity: the *or* sound • CD-ROM Cycle A (Secure developing reader) resource sheet 2.4: plot of E.T. in correct order • Student Book page 34-35: plot and film still of E.T.	• to be able to read simple unfamiliar texts accurately • to be able to give a balanced retelling of a story and to retell clearly **Target areas** • Target area 1: Finding and using textual reference • Target area 3: Understanding text layout and organisation	AF2, AF3, AF4

Starter (15 minutes)

Show students the different letter combinations that make the *or* sound by underlining and identifying the letters that represent the phoneme in the following words: *wall, walk, crawl, law, haul, August, more, door, for, four, war, caught*. Emphasise how many different spellings of the phoneme there are. With students working in pairs or threes, give out copies of the phoneme chart (resource sheet 2.1) or display one on a projector. Give out sets of word cards or use a class set for students to arrange on a projector (resource sheet 2.2). Students sort the words by placing them in the correct column, according to the spelling of the sound. Using blank cards, students then add their own examples of words with the *or* sound – aim to get two or three in each column.

Check answers, using the teaching pages (resource sheet 2.3) on a projector. Together, generate strategies for remembering which spelling of the phoneme is needed in the following words: *awful, thought, caught/court, four, talk*. Stress that as well as getting the word looking right, students might need to use a mnemonic or to highlight the difficult part of the word. You could draw up strategies together and record them.

Introduction (15 minutes)

Explain the purpose of the lesson, which is to sequence the events of a story in the correct order and to retell the story clearly. Write the following sentences on the whiteboard: *An alien is stranded on earth. A young boy finds him and they become friends. After many adventures, the alien returns home.* Ask students how they know that this story is told in the correct order and together highlight the "clues" that readers use to check logical sequence, e.g. main characters introduced (*an alien, a young boy*) then pronouns used which refer back to these characters (*him, they*); logical order of actions (*is stranded, is found, returns home*); time connectives (*after*). Ask students if they recognise this story and direct them to pages 34–35 of the Student Book, looking together at the image and plot outline for E.T. Give the students the story extracts, jumbled up from Resource Sheet 2.4. Ask them to scan the jumbled events of the story and see how quickly they can locate the first sentence (*A family of aliens land on earth*) and the last sentence (*E.T. is reunited with his family and has to say goodbye to his earth friends*) Highlight the clues they used to decide e.g. first mention of characters (family of aliens); repetition of *family* and *earth*; the word *reunited*.

Development (20 minutes)

Students work in pairs to sequence the rest of the sentences. Encourage them to re-read frequently and to think about the clues they are using to decide the correct order for the events in the story. Show Resource 2.4 to establish the correct sequence. You may prefer to cut up this resource on acetate strips and use them to model the sequencing activity, rehearsing with students the clues you are using. Once sequenced, encourage students to retell the story, this time adding more detail to events and characters. Model this for them first, then divide students into pairs or threes and give each group one of the sentences to expand. It would be helpful to give them a time limit e.g. one minute, so they can practise adding enough detail and rehearsing their telling.

Reading for meaning in fiction texts, supporting ideas with evidence from the text

Cycle A

Duration: 1 hour

Plenary (10 minutes)
Hear the whole story told in sequence round the class. Reflect and take feedback: was the order of events clear and easy to follow? Did the story hold your interest?
Extension activity
Practise telling the story of another science fiction film you know. Your aim is to sequence events and retell them in a clear and logical order.

Lesson Plan 3 of 3

Reading for meaning in fiction texts, supporting ideas with evidence from the text

Secure developing reader

Cycle A

Duration: 1 hour

Resources needed	Lesson aims	Assessment Focuses
• CD-ROM Cycle A (Secure developing reader) resource sheet 3.1: starter activity revising the *ar* and *or* sounds, one copy per student • Student Book page 37: cards with prompts for reading images • Student Book pages 36–37: image and screenplay from *Star Wars* • blank A5 cards, five per group of four or five	• to be able to give a balanced retelling of a story and to retell clearly • to be able to comment on a story's main characters, using evidence from the text **Target areas** • Target area 1: Finding and using textual reference • Target area 2: Skimming and scanning • Target area 3: Understanding text layout and organisation	AF2, AF3, AF4

Starter (15 minutes)

Using resource sheet 3.1, revise spelling choices for the *ar* and *or* sounds. Read the extract aloud, with students following. Read it again, asking students to highlight all the words in which they can hear the *ar* sound: display and check.

Read the extract again, this time asking students to highlight all the words in which they can hear the *or* sound: display and check.

With students using mini-whiteboards, read the list of words below, pausing for students to write each one. Encourage them to write down more than one choice if they are unsure, then to consider which one looks and sounds right. Hold up final choices to show.

Word list: *part, heart, harm, charm, calm*; *store, claw, talk, awful, tour*.

Introduction (15 minutes)

Using the prompt cards on page 37 of the student book, ask students to question the *Star Wars* image. Pool ideas about what kind of characters and events they would expect from a film in which this was an important image.

Explain that they are going to read an extract from the screenplay for *Star Wars*. Get the students to skim the text to locate headings, use of capital letters, layout of speech in the script. Show and explain the following terms used in the screenplay:

EXT: Exterior shot; INT: Interior shot; Rollup = summary of the story moving slowly up the screen from bottom to top (starts *War! The Republic is …* and ends with *to rescue the captive Chancellor);* *PAN* = movement of camera sweeping from side to side of action on screen or up and down; *TRACK* = camera moving alongside an object.

Ask students to scan the screenplay extract to locate these film terms and to look again at how the text is organised and structured. Get them to scan the text again for names of characters and places and sort these into 'sides' in the battle. Encourage students to locate and read complete noun phrases, e.g. *the ruthless Sith Lord, Count Dooku*; *the fiendish droid leader, General Grievous*; *a Trade Federation Droid Drop Fighter*, etc. You could list these as students find them and get students to practise saying the whole phrase fluently.

Development (20 minutes)

Students in groups of four or five divide the whole text between them and read it all the way through (or do this as a whole class if preferred). Give each group five blank A5 cards. Using the information in the text, the group's task is to create character fact cards for the following: Count Dooku; General Grievous; Chancellor Palpatine; Obi Wan and Anakin Skywalker. They should be able to use these to retell the story. The fact cards should contain main 5W facts, e.g. who the person is; what has happened to them; where they are going, etc., using relevant details and vocabulary from the

Reading for meaning in fiction texts, supporting ideas with evidence from the text

Secure developing reader

Cycle A

Duration: 1 hour

screenplay. Students can draw a suitable image to go with the facts and include a speech bubble of dialogue as appropriate.
Plenary (10 minutes)
Students practise retelling the story round the group, using the character fact cards in sequence as prompts. As a whole class, suggest the next two or three lines of dialogue between Anakin and Obi-Wan.
Extension activity
Plan what you would add to the concept map that shows more about how films depict space/science fiction.

Reading for meaning in non-fiction texts, supporting ideas with evidence from the text

Secure developing reader

Cycle B

Duration: 1 hour

Resources needed	Lesson aims	Assessment Focuses
• CD-ROM Cycle B (Secure developing reader) resource sheet 1.1: starter activity: key vocabulary for lesson cycle • CD-ROM Cycle B (Secure developing reader) resource sheet 1.2: photograph of UFO and speculation and evidence stems • Student Book pages 38–39: Do aliens exist? text	• to know how to scan a text to locate relevant information and read ahead independently • to be able to tackle unfamiliar words and be aware of strategies used to do this • to be able to extract information from non-fiction texts in answer to specific questions **Target areas** • Target area 1: Finding and using textual reference • Target area 2: Skimming and scanning • Target area 3: Understanding text layout and organisation	AF2, AF3, AF4, AF6

Starter (15 minutes)

Using resource sheet 1.1, introduce students to vocabulary for the topic by:

- sorting the words into alphabetical order, e.g. by students holding them up on a 'washing line' in the right order. Do this as a whole class or with groups of students competing in a time limit
- matching dictionary definitions to the correct word, as a whole class or in groups
- as a whole class, predicting what kind of text these words will be found in.

Vocabulary in alphabetical order: *alien, atom, comet, exist, extra-terrestrial, hoax, solar system, theory, UFO.*

Introduction (15 minutes)

Remind students of the topic for this cycle of lessons by recalling the concept map that was started in Cycle A Lesson 1. Pose the question that students will be investigating in this cycle of lessons and add it to the concept map: 'Do aliens exist?' Give students 60 seconds' thinking time to answer this question for themselves: Yes/No/Not sure + one reason. Ask them to write their answer down so they can return to it later and reconsider it in the light of the evidence they will be exploring.

Stress the importance of speculating and asking questions when considering a topic like this that has no clear-cut answer.

Show students the photograph of 'a flying saucer' (resource sheet 1.2) and direct them to the prompt questions for exploring images that were used in Cycle A (these could usefully be printed and laminated, enough for one per pair or group of three). Get students in small groups to explore the photograph by asking and answering the questions on the cards.

Remind students of the meaning of the word *hoax*, as used in the starter activity. Pool responses in answer to the question: 'Is this photograph a hoax?' Encourage students to give clear reasons based on evidence in the photograph.

Development (20 minutes)

Return to the question: 'Do aliens exist?' Introduce the speculative language stems (resource sheet 1.2), ideally as cut-up cards, laminated as a set per pair or table group of students). Model how to use the stems to answer a question and provide evidence, by returning to the photograph used previously, e.g. ***It might be that*** *the object is an aeroplane.* ***Evidence for this*** *is the bright light that looks like the aircraft landing lights.* ***Also****, the object is low in the sky as though it's a plane coming in to land at a*

Reading for meaning in non-fiction texts, supporting ideas with evidence from the text

Secure developing reader

Cycle B

Duration: 1 hour

nearby airport.

Turn to pages 38–39 in the Student Book. Read this with the students, highlighting through intonation, and by listing, the speculative words and phrases that are used in introducing the topic: **whether** we are alone in the universe *or* **whether** we've got company in the shape of aliens. **People claim** to have met aliens and seen UFOs – unidentified flying objects – and **some people even say** they've been abducted by extra terrestrials. But what do we **really** know about them – **do** they exist at all? Highlight the modal verbs in the 5W questions*: would, might*, and the use of *really* in *if aliens really exist*? Stress for students through intonation and explanation the use of rhetorical questions and their purpose, i.e. to draw us in to look for possible answers; to suggest questions that are difficult to answer.

Ask students to skim the text that follows by looking at the illustrations, headings and subheadings, and to establish what kind of text it is, e.g. in comparison to other similar layouts they have seen. Pool answers to establish the form, purpose and likely audience for the text about aliens.

Ask students in pairs to read the 'website' introduction (from 'For years people have speculated' to 'Have your say!') and to pick out speculative words and phrases that are used. Pool these as a class: *whether*, *or*, *perhaps*, *whatever*, *might* + rhetorical questions. Discuss why they are used and the effect they have on the reader, e.g. to signal that what follows might not be proven fact; to suggest that alternative views will be considered.

Plenary (10 minutes)

Return to prompts for speculation and providing evidence. Students in small groups use them to practise answering the question 'Do aliens exist?' They can use evidence from their own experience and from the information read during this lesson.

Extension activity

Devise further questions you want to ask that would help you decide whether aliens exist or not.

Lesson Plan 2 of 3

Reading for meaning in non-fiction texts, supporting ideas with evidence from the text

Secure developing reader

Cycle B

Duration: 1 hour

Resources needed	Lesson aims	Assessment Focuses
• CD-ROM Cycle B (Secure developing reader) resource sheet 2.1: recording sheet • Student Book pages 38–39: webpage about life on other planets	• to know how to scan a text to locate relevant information and read ahead independently • to be able to tackle unfamiliar words and be aware of strategies used to do this • to be able to extract information from non-fiction texts in answer to specific questions **Target areas** • Target area 1: Finding and using textual reference • Target area 2: Skimming and scanning • Target area 3: Understanding text layout and organisation	AF2, AF3, AF5

Starter (15 minutes)

Remind students of the modal verbs that are used to express possibility: *might, can, could, should, shall, will, must, would*. Generate lists of rhyming words for each modal, to emphasise patterns in spelling, e.g. *might – fright – tight – right – night; must – trust – dust – crust*. Point out other vowel phoneme choices that might cause confusion, e.g. *w<u>oo</u>d* for *w<u>oul</u>d* but the fact that *should/could/would* are all spelt in the same way. Practise substituting them in different sentences to bring out the differences in meaning, e.g. 'I might/can/could/should/shall/will/must/would do my homework tonight.' Get students to generate their own sentences in which modals can be used and to decide a rank order from the weakest to the strongest possibility.

Introduction (15 minutes)

Remind students of the research question 'Do aliens exist?' Explain that they will be working in home and expert groups in this lesson to find answers to this question and to pool the information they find. Direct them to page 38 of the Student Book and show the 5W questions they will be using to find specific information:

- Who has seen evidence that aliens exist?
- What might aliens look like?
- When have aliens been spotted?
- Where could aliens be from?
- Why is it hard to be sure if aliens really exist?

Organise students into 'home groups' of five. Get each group to discuss initial answers to these questions, based on what they already know about the topic. They can record initial ideas on the recording sheet (resource sheet 2.1). Stress that they will be adding further information to this planning sheet when they next join as a home group.

Development (20 minutes)

Re-organise students into 'expert groups' containing one member of each of the home groups. Allocate each expert group one of the research questions so that they are all covered. Direct students to pages 38–39 of the Student Book, information from a website investigation into whether aliens exist. Ask expert groups to scan the text for subheadings and key words that will help them answer their question and then to close read the relevant sections. Remind them how to use the 5W stems to help the search, e.g. by looking for dates and names. Model for them how to scan ahead in a sentence to locate the main idea, e.g. by using the following example from the text: **According to experts,** *if*

Reading for meaning in non-fiction texts, supporting ideas with evidence from the text

Secure developing reader

Cycle B

Duration: 1 hour

aliens do exist ***they are*** *more likely to be* ***small*** *and look* ***like worms or other bugs.*** Point out the main verb, how the pronoun *they* refers back to aliens and the key words describing what they look like.

Give time for expert groups to agree an answer to their question, based on what they have read. Support individuals or groups as needed.

Plenary (10 minutes)

Students return to their home groups and take it in turns to report what they have discovered in answer to each question. They should record this in the appropriate place on the recording sheet.

Ask: 'As a result of your research, have you changed your ideas? Has anything you've discovered surprised you?'

Extension activity

Review how well you worked in your home and expert groups in this lesson.

Lesson Plan 3 of 3

Reading for meaning in non-fiction texts, supporting ideas with evidence from the text

Secure developing reader

Cycle B

Duration: 1 hour

Resources needed	Lesson aims	Assessment Focuses
• CD-ROM Cycle B (Secure developing reader) resource sheet 3.1: starter activity: scientific suffixes and prefixes • CD-ROM Cycle B (Secure developing reader) resource sheet 3.2: empathy prompts and stems • Student Book pages 40–41: 'Do aliens exist? Have your say' text • post-it notes	• to be able to tackle unfamiliar words and be aware of strategies used to do this • to be able to extract information from non-fiction texts in answer to specific questions **Target areas** • Target area 1: Finding and using textual reference • Target area 4: Using empathy to make judgement	AF2, AF3, AF6

Starter (15 minutes)

Using resource sheet 3.1, show students how to build a word web using suffixes and prefixes that are common in scientific words. Point out the meaning of the prefix or suffix and encourage students to work out what *geo* and *bio* mean ('earth' and 'life'). You can get students to make up plausible words to add to the web, e.g. *photogeograph* – a picture of the Earth taken from space; *photologist* – someone who studies light.

Devise more word webs using any of the following prefixes and suffixes and their meanings: *meter* (measure); *super* (much); *phone* (sound); *micro* (small); *scope* (see/sight).

Introduction (15 minutes)

Introduce the word *empathy* and show students how it is linked to *sympathy* and *apathy*, i.e. the *pathy* suffix comes from *pathos*, meaning 'feelings'; *empathising* means 'having feelings towards or about someone or something'. Explain that empathising is an important reading strategy because it helps us to understand someone else's ideas and emotions and to respond to them as a reader: we might like or dislike a character in a story, or agree or disagree with a view that has been expressed. Explain that they are also building skills in providing evidence for their responses, by referring to details from the text. Getting better at reading includes being able to respond to what they have read and back up what they think with detailed evidence.

Display or give out the empathy prompt questions and phrases (resource sheet 3.2). Clarify with students the words and phrases that are useful for agreeing and adding their own opinions, and those which are useful for disagreeing and offering alternative views.

Development (20 minutes)

Turn to pages 40–41 in the Student Book: 'Do aliens exist? Have your say' (students' opinions about life on other planets). Remind students how to highlight the main clause within a longer sentence in order to get to the heart of the meaning. Model this again if necessary on the first example. Encourage students to give a very short 'title' to the extract that sums up what the writer is saying.

Students take each opinion in turn and use the prompt empathy questions to respond to it. They should then use the words and phrases prompts to compose a 'reply' to each person's opinion.

Finally, they should decide their own opinion on the topic and use the prompts to help them write it on a post it note which can be pinned to the class concept map.

Plenary (10 minutes)

Ask students to return to the statement they originally wrote down in answer to 'Do aliens exist?' In the light of evidence explored in the last few lessons, have they changed their minds? Give individual thinking time, then discuss in pairs, using the stems: *At first I thought … because. … Now I think …*

Reading for meaning in non-fiction texts, supporting ideas with evidence from the text

Secure developing reader

Cycle B

Duration: 1 hour

because … Recap use of prompt questions, words and phrases during these lessons. Which have they found the most helpful? Where else could students use them to help explore meaning?
Extension activity
Build the longest answer you can to the question 'Do aliens exist?'

Lesson Plan 1 of 3

Reading for meaning in fiction texts, supporting ideas with evidence from the text

Secure developing reader

Cycle C

Duration: 1 hour

Resources needed	Lesson aims	Assessment Focuses
• CD-ROM Cycle C (Secure developing reader) resource sheet 1.1: starter activity • mini-whiteboards • CD-ROM Cycle C (Secure developing reader) resource sheets 1.2 : prompts for speculation and prediction and 1.3: modelling a PEE paragraph • Student Book pages 42–43: images from versions of *The War of the Worlds*	• to know how to comment on some of the ways in which a text is written or presented • to be able to respond to questions which invite speculation and prediction • to know how to use expression and intonation to enhance meaning when reading **Target areas** • Target area 1: Finding and using textual reference • Target area 4: Using empathy to make judgements	AF3, AF5, AF6

Starter (15 minutes)

The aim of the starter activity is to identify when consonants double if the suffixes *-ing* and *-ed* are added. Students write **long** on one side of their mini-whiteboard; **short** on the other side. Read out the list of words below and ask students to say if the vowel sound is long or short, by holding up the right side of their board. Model an example: *hop* (short vowel sound); *gate* (long vowel sound). Alternate between short sounds in: *snap, flap, shock, must, cost, lot* and long sounds in: *wait, teeth, leak, gate, bone, tune*. Using resource sheet 1.1, show the grid, getting students to say each word and identify whether the vowel sound is short or long. Ask students in pairs to discuss and decide what has happened to the final consonant each time when *-ing* is added. Can they see a pattern emerging? Encourage them to see that short vowels double the final consonant when *-ing* is added, and long vowels do not. Decide which of the words above form a past tense by adding *-ed* and whether the doubling rule still applies (*snapped, stopped*). Show the short story on the same page and ask students to read the words aloud, then choose the correct spelling for the missing words, following the convention outlined above.

Introduction (15 minutes)

Direct students to pages 42–43 of the Student Book, images of *The War of the Worlds*. Remind them of the prompts for speculation and prediction used in the previous lesson cycle. In pairs, students use prompts to help them discuss and decide an answer to the question: 'From these images, what do you think happens in the story?' Each pair joins with another pair to compare answers.

Using resource sheet 1.3, show on a projector the PEE paragraph model for making comments about texts and analysing their effects. Use the stems on resource sheet 1.2 to model how to make a simple PEE statement in answer to the question the students have just been considering.

As a class, compose another simple PEE paragraph that makes a new point and offers new evidence, e.g. POINT: I wonder whether the story will be quite violent and frightening. EVIDENCE: Evidence for this is the vivid orange, red and blue colours used in the images. EXPLANATION: These colours look harsh and disturbing and are often linked with danger and death or something mysterious.

Development (20 minutes)

Display on the whiteboard (or print on cards that are given as a set per pair of students) the following verbs: *coiled, wriggled, bulged, glistened, quivered, panted, heaved, pulsated, gripped, swayed.*

For each one, invite students to explain what kind of movement is being described and to predict what kind of creature might move in this way. List synonyms for each verb where this is helpful to clarify meaning, or use illustrations. Encourage students to say each word clearly and with expression. Insert 'the thing' at the start of the list and get students to read all the verbs in a variety of ways, as if they are retelling the story of a sighting of a strange creature: they could whisper to a partner, shout some

Lesson Plan 1 of 3

Reading for meaning in fiction texts, supporting ideas with evidence from the text

Secure developing reader

Cycle C

Duration: 1 hour

words as if frightened, hiss them, etc. Regroup the words as liked to emphasise and exaggerate their sounds, e.g. sorting by short or long vowels or by soft and hard consonant sounds.

As a class, compose a short poem entitled 'The Thing', using some of these verbs as a starting point. Encourage students to change verbs to include both *-ing* and *-ed* endings. Invite suggestions for adding similes and adjectives: model and compose together first, then ask students to continue in pairs, e.g.

The thing ...
Coiled tight as a snake
Bulging as if it had swallowed its prey.
Panting, it heaved itself over the ground.
etc.

Plenary (10 minutes)

Students read their poems aloud, either to the whole class or in a small group, concentrating on using intonation to emphasise meaning. Choose one example for the whole class to work on. Using the prompts for speculation and prediction, ask students to suggest what this creature from *The War of the Worlds* will look like and what it might do in the story. Encourage them to refer to specific words as evidence, e.g. 'Perhaps the creature will actually be like a snake and it might kill humans by crushing them to death. I think this because of the words "coiled" and "gripped", which make me think of a python or a boa constrictor.'

Extension activity

Draw the creature described in your poem.

Lesson Plan 2 of 3

Reading for meaning in fiction texts, supporting ideas with evidence from the text

Secure developing reader

Cycle C

Duration: 1 hour

Resources needed	Lesson aims	Assessment Focuses
• CD-ROM Cycle C (Secure developing reader) resource sheet 2.1: noun phrases • Student Book page 43: description of Martian emerging from cylinder	• to know how to comment on some of the ways in which a text is written or presented • to be able to comment on a story's main characters using evidence from the text • to be able to respond to questions about feelings created by the story **Target areas** • Target area 1: Finding and using textual reference • Target area 2: Skimming and scanning • Target area 4: Using empathy to make judgements	AF2, AF3, AF5

Starter (15 minutes)

Give the students a spelling test using the verbs that were focused on in the previous lesson: *coiled, wriggled, bulged, glistened, quivered, panted, heaved, pulsated, gripped, swayed.* Help by reminding them of the *-ed* ending that all these verbs have, and by encouraging them to repeat each word to emphasise each phoneme. Ask them to highlight any part of the word they are unsure of, and to make several attempts if needed, showing on mini-whiteboards or on paper what each choice was. When you give the correct spellings, encourage students to show the 'best guesses' they have made. As a class, decide which words might need extra attention and work out which spelling strategies will be most helpful in remembering the correct spelling.

Introduction (15 minutes)

Remind students of the speculations and predictions they made about the creature from Mars in the last lesson. Using resource sheet 2.1, introduce more vocabulary from the description of the Martian in *The War of the Worlds*, this time concentrating on how noun phrases are built up. On a projector, uncover the lines in turn, explaining how the writer places detail before and after the noun. Show students how they need to read backwards and forwards around the noun to secure the meaning. Uncover the complete complex sentence and ask students to scan ahead to find the main nouns and verbs, then to read it aloud, using the punctuation to emphasise meaning and to read with expression. As a class, build a new noun phrase together, starting with *mouth*, inviting suggestions for what the Martian's mouth might look like, then compare with the original version: *a peculiar V-shaped* ***mouth*** *under the eyes, with a pointed upper lip.*

Development (20 minutes)

Direct the students to page 43 of the Student Book, the description of the Martian emerging from the cylinder. Ask them to scan the whole extract looking for: a) the verbs that will be familiar to them from work in the last two lessons and b) the noun phrases that they have just been working on. Then ask them to skim-read the extract by reading the first sentence of each paragraph and the last two sentences of the extract. Give students time to read each paragraph 'in their heads', then read the whole extract aloud, sharing it between students as appropriate.

Prepare and then share responses to the questions: 'Is this what you expected a Martian to look like? Which details do you most remember and why?'

Feed back responses to these questions by modelling short PEE answers on the whiteboard and asking students to create their own PEE answers orally, e.g. 'The Martians seem to be huge creatures, much bigger than humans. They are "the size of a bear". Their size makes them move slowly and they

Reading for meaning in fiction texts, supporting ideas with evidence from the text

Secure developing reader

Cycle C

Duration: 1 hour

seem quite clumsy so perhaps the humans will be able to run away from them.'

Emphasise how evidence from the text is being used to infer and deduce meaning. You can scaffold this activity in various ways, e.g. by giving students a point and asking them to find evidence to support it; by providing a short quotation from the text and asking students to explain what it shows us; by asking True/False questions and asking students to quote the evidence used in deciding an answer.

Plenary (10 minutes)

Recap what the students have discovered so far about the way the Martian from the cylinder looks and moves. Remind them of the word *empathy* and its meaning, and how *empathising* is a useful reading strategy because it helps to put us 'in the shoes' of characters in a story. If they were in the crowd gathered around the cylinder as the Martian emerged, what would they be thinking? How would they feel? Together, devise a set of empathy prompt questions, then try them out in pairs, one student asking the question, e.g. in role as a radio or TV journalist, the other giving the response, supported by details from the text.

Suggested prompt questions: 'Why were you in the crowd in the first place? What did you see first when the lid fell off? Was it what you expected to see? When were you most scared and why? How did the people around you react? What will you never forget?'

Extension activity

Think about the details from the description that you most remember and why these details are memorable.

Lesson Plan 3 of 3

Reading for meaning in fiction texts, supporting ideas with evidence from the text

Secure developing reader

Cycle C

Duration: 1 hour

Resources needed	Lesson aims	Framework Objectives
• Student Book page 43: description of Martian emerging from cylinder • CD-ROM Cycle C (Secure developing reader) resource sheet 3.1: labelled drawing for retelling story	• to be able to give a balanced retelling of a story and to retell clearly • to be able to respond to questions about feelings created by the story **Target areas** • Target area 1: Finding and using textual reference • Target area 4: Using empathy to make judgements	Y7: R2, R6, **R8** Y8: R4, **R5** **Assessment Focuses** AF2, AF3, AF5, AF6

Starter (15 minutes)

List the following adjectives on the whiteboard, or show them on cards: *worried, nervous, anxious, scared, frightened, alarmed, terrified, horrified, petrified.* Get students to read each one aloud clearly and clarify any difficulties by applying appropriate decoding strategies, e.g. chunking into syllables and phonemes, relating to other, known words, highlighting common endings. Agree an explanation of how the words are linked, e.g. all describe fear.

Ask students to sequence them in order of mildest to strongest response; they can do this in pairs and compare with other groups. Hear several versions of an order (it isn't necessary to agree on a definitive one). Encourage students to say each word clearly as they decide on an order. You can extend this activity by getting students to suggest other synonyms for describing fear, and to place them on the continuum. You could also ask students to use each word in a sentence that will bring out its meaning.

Introduction (15 minutes)

Read the third paragraph of the extract on page 43 of the Student Book aloud to the students, asking them to locate words and phrases that show how the onlookers react to seeing the Martian emerge from the cylinder. Clarify what these responses show, e.g. by asking students to complete statements with evidence from the text: 'Which words show that he was terrified? What made the onlooker "shriek with terror"? Which detail sounds most horrific?'

Explain that their task in small groups is to retell the story of the Martian sighting, from the first-person point of view of an onlooker, and that the aim is to describe events in a clear sequence and using lots of detail. They will use a labelled drawing as a prompt or 'script' for their retelling of the story.

Show students the drawing on resource sheet 3.1 and point out the noun phrases and verbs used to label it. Model for students how to retell the story of this episode, using the labelled drawing as a prompt and retelling the story in the first person, e.g. *When I looked at the cylinder, I could see that nearly two feet of shining metal screw was sticking up. Someone – or something – was unscrewing the lid from inside. Then it fell off with a loud clang and a Thing started to climb out ...*

An alternative approach would be to give students the list of phrases from the extract which they use to direct you in constructing a labelled drawing on the whiteboard. The class then use this to retell the story.

Development (20 minutes)

Ask students in pairs or threes to continue retelling the story in this way, using the labelled drawing to prompt them and adding their own details to fill in the story.

Now tell them that as eyewitnesses of the event, they are going to be interviewed 'live' on radio to give an account of what they saw. They will have exactly 60 seconds of broadcast time. Get students to rehearse a timed retelling, stressing the following features as success criteria: make the sequence of events clear to the listener; describe the most frightening details about the Martians' appearance;

Reading for meaning in fiction texts, supporting ideas with evidence from the text

Cycle C

Duration: 1 hour

explain to listeners how you and others felt about seeing the Martian.

Plenary (10 minutes)

Hear a selection of 60-second broadcasts. Gather feedback based on the success criteria, e.g. two positives (WWW: what worked well); one thing to do differently (EBI: even better if).

Remind students of the reading strategies they have been using during this cycle and clarify understanding of what they refer to: predicting and speculating; empathising, supporting ideas with evidence from the text. Ask students to assess their use of these strategies, using the WWW/EBI formula described above.

Extension activity

Predict and speculate about what might happen next in the story.

Lesson Plan 1 of 3

Make judgements about texts, supported by evidence

Secure developing reader

Cycle D

Duration: 1 hour

Resources needed	Lesson aims	Assessment Focuses
• CD-ROM Cycle D (Secure developing reader) resource sheet 1.1a: starter activity, sorting words in different ways, and 1.1b: answers • CD-ROM Cycle D (Secure developing reader) resource sheet 1.2: image response cards (if needed as separate resource; also in Student Book pages 44–45) • Student Book pages 46–49: extracts from *Moon Landing* • CD-ROM Cycle D (Secure developing reader) resource sheets 1.3: template for newspaper report and 1.4: items to cut up and arrange	• to know how to comment on some of the ways in which a text is written or presented • to be able to express opinions and make judgements **Target areas** • Target area 1: Finding and using textual reference • Target area 3: Understanding text layout and organisation • Target area 4: Using empathy to make judgements	AF2, AF3, AF4, AF6

Starter (15 minutes)

Using resource sheet 1.1a, introduce key words for the topic by asking students to sort them in different ways. This can be done as a whole-class, individual or paired activity, as appropriate. Use this as a chance to recap with students about phonic choices and ways of approaching 'unseen' words. Answers are provided on resource sheet 1.1b. Ask students to predict what the text will be about, based on these key words. You can extend this by asking them to speculate about the 'story' of the text, by combining the key vocabulary in different ways, e.g. 'Astronauts launch from Earth in a rocket on a mission to be the first men to land and walk on the Moon.'

Introduction (15 minutes)

Share ideas about how people have imagined the Moon and examples of sayings about it (e.g. 'it's made of cheese', 'once in a blue moon'; to be 'over the moon' about something, etc.) and speculate about why we might have such a fascination with the Moon. Ask if they know any details about the mission to put the first men on the Moon, e.g. the names of the people and the spacecraft involved.

Direct students to the photograph of Neil Armstrong on the Moon on page 49 of the Student Book. In pairs, get them to discuss the image by asking and answering the questions on two of the response cards: 'Visualising' and 'Predicting and speculating' (resource sheet 1.2). Take brief feedback.

Development (20 minutes)

Explain to students that in this cycle of lessons they will be taking on the role of journalists, investigating and reporting information about the first Moon landing. Draw out what they think journalists need to be good at, e.g. asking questions, reporting facts accurately, including interesting details, interviewing eyewitnesses and summarising what they say. Using resource sheet 1.3, first display the template for a newspaper report on a projector. Ask: 'What kind of text is shown here and how do we know?' You could illustrate the key features of a front-page newspaper report by filling in the template with the outline of a contemporary news story. Display the cut-up items on resource sheet 1.4 and with students' help, use them to reconstruct the front page for the day the US astronauts landed on the Moon. Label each item, using the strips showing key terms.

Plenary (10 minutes)

Discuss with students why they think a front-page news report is arranged in this way. Ask: 'What is the impact on the reader of the presentational devices used?' (the headline catches the attention and

Make judgements about texts, supported by evidence

Secure developing reader

Cycle D

Duration: 1 hour

sums up the story in a very few words; the subheadings mark out the key stages in the story; the image is chosen to catch the eye and appeal to the reader's imagination or feelings). As a class, skim the text on pages 46–49 of the Student Book, looking just at the photographs and the subheadings that mark the main stages of the story. Based on the ideas and information gathered by doing this, ask the students to suggest alternative headlines for the *Daily Moon* front page and share examples, e.g. 'The *Eagle* has landed'; 'A giant step for mankind'; 'Moon mission triumph', etc. Which do they think is the best headline and why?

Extension activity

Ask a range of older adults what they remember about the first Moon landing and what they thought about it. Record some of the things they say in the form of 'soundbites' (i.e. short, punchy statements) that you can tell others in your class.

Lesson Plan
2 of 3

Make judgements about texts, supported by evidence

Secure developing reader

Cycle D

Duration: 1 hour

Resources needed	Lesson aims	Assessment Focuses
• CD-ROM Cycle D Secure developing reader) resource sheet 2.1: starter activity on punctuation • CD-ROM Cycle D (Secure developing reader) resource sheet 2.2: Moon landing extract. • Student Book pages 44–45: To the moon • Student Book pages 46–47: extract from *Moon Landing*	• to know how to scan for and locate relevant information in answer to specific questions • to be able to extract information from non-fiction text for a specific purpose **Target areas** • Target area 1: Finding and using textual reference • Target area 3: Understanding text layout and organisation	AF2, AF3, AF4, AF5, AF6

Starter (15 minutes)

Display the following punctuation marks prominently on the whiteboard and provide labels as students name them. Remind them of the function of these punctuation marks:

"..." speech marks or quotation marks, used to show the words spoken by someone or when words from a text are written down.

! exclamation mark, used to stress an idea or emphasise emotion e.g. surprise, humour, anger

... ellipsis, used to show a pause, for example to create tension or drama

– a dash, used one at a time or in a pair, to show a pause or to emphasise when extra information is added.

Give pairs or small groups of students the set of cards on resource sheet 2.1. Get them to read them aloud, using the punctuation to suggest the tone of voice they need to use. Model this for them as needed. Then ask them to sequence the extracts in chronological (time) order (cards arranged in the correct sequence shown on resource sheet 2.1), and to read them aloud round the group in this order, with intonation and expression that will bring out the excitement and drama of the story. Hear one or two 'performances'. Remind students that writers use punctuation to help the reader decide *how* to say the words and to choose the right tone of voice.

Introduction (15 minutes)

Remind them of their role as journalists who are investigating the story of the first Moon landing in order to report on it. Look again at the image of Neil Armstrong on the Moon and together read the prompts on the four cards on pages 44–45 of the Student Book. As a whole class, draw up a set of 5W questions for investigation as you read the first half of the account of the Moon landing.

Provide model questions for students as needed, e.g. 'When was the rocket launched? Where was the launch site? Who with Neil Armstrong on this mission? What was the rocket called? Why did people watching the launch cry?'

Remind students how to skim and scan for information in a text by looking at picture clues, headings and side headings, key nouns that tell you what the subject is, and by reading the first and last sentences in paragraphs. Model these strategies for them, on a section of the text, then ask them to use them independently on the first half of the text.

See how many of the students' 5W questions have already been answered during this first skim-reading.

Development (20 minutes)

Close read the first half of the text together (Student book pages 46–47 or resource sheet 2.2 page1). Divide up the reading in order to emphasise the drama of the account and to stress how students can

Make judgements about texts, supported by evidence

Cycle D

Duration: 1 hour

use punctuation to read for meaning, e.g. using all voices in the class to read the countdown to the launch, with the teacher narrating in between; using confident readers to take the parts of the astronauts and mission control.

Ask students to tell back the 'bare bones' of the account so far, to check understanding of chronology and key events. Answer any remaining 5W questions.

Display the front-page newspaper template (resource sheet 1.3) and insert the *Daily Moon* masthead. Students in role as journalists suggest the following: a suitable summary headline for events so far; an image and caption. Take suggestions and choose one idea, writing in details on the template. Write in the first subheading: 'Lift Off!' With students' help, model how to write the first part of the report, including 5W information, e.g. *At 9.27 yesterday morning, history was made when the* Saturn V *rocket blasted off from its launch site in Houston. On board were astronauts Neil Armstrong and Buzz Aldrin, about to become the first humans to set foot on the surface of the Moon.* Invite students to check back in the text to make sure details are accurate.

Write in the second subheading: 'One small step,' and ask students working together to compose the next few sentences of the report to match the subheading, checking back in the text for details.

Plenary (10 minutes)

Hear suggestions for this part of the report and use them to write a summary of events onto the report, e.g. *109 hours after lift-off, the small spacecraft called the* Eagle *touched down on the Moon's surface. Armstrong was the first to leave the craft, watched by millions of people around the world on TV.* Ask students to find in the text the words spoken by Armstrong and use them to end the report, e.g. *As he set foot on the Moon, Armstrong said: 'One small step for a man. One giant leap for mankind.'*

Read the whole report and ask students to judge whether it sounds like a realistic news report.

Extension activity

Ask a range of people if they can complete the words spoken by Neil Armstrong: 'One small step for a man …'

Make sure you can tell them what comes next, in case they don't know.

Lesson Plan
3 of 3

Make judgements about texts, supported by evidence

Secure developing reader

Cycle D

Duration: 1 hour

Resources needed	Lesson aims	Assessment Focuses
• Student Book pages 44–45 image of astronaut on Moon and prompt questions • CD-ROM Cycle D (Secure developing reader) resource sheet 3.1: starter activity • CD-ROM Cycle D (Secure developing reader) resource sheet 2.2: extract from *Moon Landing* • CD-ROM Cycle D (Secure developing reader) resource sheet 1.3: template for newspaper report • Student Book pages 48–49: *Moon Landing* extract	• to know how to scan for and locate relevant information in answer to specific questions • to be able to extract information from non-fiction text for a specific purpose • to be able to express opinions and make judgements **Target areas** • Target area 1: Finding and using textual reference • Target area 3: Understanding text layout and organisation • Target area 4: Using empathy to make judgements	AF2, AF3, AF5, AF6

Starter (15 minutes)

Display the following quotation from the text: 'His voice is electric with tension.' Discuss with students what this shows us about Neil Armstrong's emotions when he steps onto the surface of the Moon for the first time and speaks to mission control in Houston. Direct students to resource sheet 3.1. Complete the activity as a whole class or in pairs who report back, as you think appropriate.

Introduction (15 minutes)

Look for a final time at the image of Neil Armstrong on the Moon (pages 44–45 in the Student Book), and together read the prompts on the 'Empathising' card (labelled with the heart icon). Draw up a set of questions that students want to ask Neil Armstrong about his experience, e.g. 'What was the most exciting part of the mission? Were you frightened at any point? How did you feel when you left the Moon?' etc. Ask them to look out for details of his feelings and thoughts when they read the second half of the text. Ask students to skim-read the second part of the text on pages 48–49 (or use page 2 of resource sheet 2.2), using the strategies rehearsed in the last lesson. Can they now answer any of their 'empathy' questions?

Development (20 minutes)

Close read the second half of the text together. As before, divide up the reading in order to emphasise the drama of the account and to stress how students can use punctuation to read for meaning, e.g. using all voices in the class to read short sentences such as 'There's no time to think', 'His voice is electric with tension' or the sections in speech marks. Again, ask students to tell back the 'bare bones' of the rest of the account, to check understanding of chronology and key events. Share responses to empathy questions, clarifying with reasons from the text whether or not they would want to be in Armstrong's shoes.

Supply pairs or threes with a new copy of the template for a front-page news report (resource sheet 1.3). Display the model from the last lesson on the whiteboard. The students' task is to provide a news report of the events in the second half of the text. They will need to supply a headline, a description of an image and a caption, two subheadings and two or three sentences of the story under each subheading. Provide subheadings if needed, e.g. 'Probing the Moon', 'Return to Earth'.

Plenary (10 minutes)

Hear/display finished reports. Give each other feedback in answer to the questions: 'Does this sound like a real news report? Why? If we were to leave the final word to Neil Armstrong, what might he say that would sum up his experience?' Take and display some suggestions, e.g. 'When he arrived home,

Lesson Plan
3 of 3

Make judgements about texts, supported by evidence

Secure developing reader

Cycle D

Duration: 1 hour

Armstrong said: "Nothing I do will ever be as exciting as walking on the Moon."'
Extension activity
Look at a front-page newspaper report. Can you find the following features: masthead, headline, an image and caption, subheadings, columns?

Lesson Plan 1 of 3

Make judgements about texts, supporting ideas with evidence

Secure developing reader

Assessment

Duration: 1 hour

Resources needed	Lesson aims	Assessment Focuses
• Teacher's Guide page 68: starter activity, 'Writers' effects' • Teacher's Guide pages 68–70: Assessment Task 1 and mark scheme • Student Book page 46–49: 'Moon landing' text	• to know how to scan for and locate relevant information in answer to specific questions • to be able to extract information from a text for a specific purpose • to be able to express an opinion about a text **Target areas** • Target area 1: Finding and using textual reference • Target area 4: Using empathy to make judgements	AF2, AF3, AF5

Starter (15 minutes)

Explain to students what AF5 for reading asks them to do: to give an opinion about how a writer uses particular words and phrases for effect or impact on the reader. Ask: 'If you were writing about someone running away from danger, what words could you use instead of 'ran' that would give a better idea of speed and fear?' Gather some synonyms and put them into a sentence, e.g. instead of *The man ran down the road*, we could use *raced, fled, shot, dashed, pounded*, etc. Display the chart (page 69 of the Teacher's Guide), one line at a time, to show the differences between the writer's first attempt and the revised one. Get the students to explain in as much detail as they can how the sentences have been changed and why the second version is better than the first. Direct them to the prompt phrases on the page and practise using them together to comment on why particular words have been chosen. Highlight these words clearly for students as they speak about them, e.g. 'When the writer says "fingers of flame" I can see the flames curling out of the rocket.'

Introduction (15 minutes)

Display the learning objective for the next three lessons: to be able to make judgements about texts, supporting ideas with evidence. Explain that in this lesson they will be working in pairs on a familiar text, to gain confidence in making judgements and supporting ideas with evidence, before working more independently on unfamiliar texts in the following two lessons. The topic of the fiction and non-fiction texts will be familiar as they are connected by the theme of space and science fiction.

Give students individual copies of the Assessment Task (see page 69 of the Teacher's Guide) and read the questions with them, checking understanding. Stress that there is no fixed answer to the second part of question 4 or to question 5: they are being asked for their opinion and can strengthen that by referring to, or quoting from, the text.

Students can work individually or in pairs on this task. Direct students to pages 46–49 of the Student Book, the text about the Moon landing that is very familiar to them. Get them to scan the text with the questions in front of them so that they can see which parts of the text they need to close read in order to find the answers. Remind them how to put quotation marks around words and phrases they quote as evidence.

Development (20 minutes)

Students complete the Assessment Task. Teacher to intervene only as needed.

Plenary (10 minutes)

Pairs exchange answers and use the answer sheet (Teacher's Guide page 71) to mark each other's assessments and provide feedback.

You can choose whether or not you want to include this task as part of your teacher assessment of

Make judgements about texts, supporting ideas with evidence

Assessment

Duration: 1 hour

students as secure developing readers. You may want to see how weaker students have coped with it, in order to inform decisions about the level of support needed for the next Assessment Task.
Extension activity
Students should self-assess the task, applying the mark scheme to their own answers.

Secure developing reader

Starter activity: writers' effects

The rocket gives off a lot of heat.	White-hot fingers of flame reach out from the rocket.
There is a lot of smoke in the air.	Blankets of smoke roll into the air.
Everyone stares at the computer screens.	Hundreds of eyes are glued to flickering computer screens.
Seen from the Moon, the Earth looks very small.	The Earth sweeps over the Moon's cratered horizon like a small blue and white marble.

When the writer says "…" I can see …

The word "…" makes me feel …

I like the part where it says "…" because …

I think …

Secure developing reader

Assessment Task 1: Moon landing

Name ______________________________ Date ______________

1. When the rocket blasted off from Earth, how did the crowd react? Look for three things they did.

____

____

____

(2 marks)

2. When the *Eagle* landed on the Moon, how was everyone at mission control in Houston feeling? Quote the words that tell you.

____

____

____

(3 marks)

3. When Neil Armstrong first backed out of the *Eagle* spacecraft and climbed down the ladder onto the Moon, what was he feeling? Which words tell you?

____

____

____

(4 marks)

4. List all the things the astronauts left behind them on the Moon. Do you think they should have left all these things?

____

____

____

____

(5 marks)

5. Read again the last part of the text, from 'The astronauts push the precious samples – 22 kg of moon rocks – into the *Eagle* …' to the end of the text.

a Why does the writer use the word 'precious' to describe the samples of moon rocks?

____

____

(2 marks)

b Why does the writer say the Earth is like 'a small blue and white marble'?

____

____

(2 marks)

Secure developing reader

Assessment Task 1: Moon landing answers

Name ______________________ Date ____________

1. When the rocket blasted off from Earth, how did the crowd react? Look for three things they did.

(AF2; 3 marks)

The crowd gasps — 1 mark
They yell, 'GO, GO, GO!' — 1 mark
Some people cry — 1 mark

2. When the *Eagle* landed on the Moon, how was everyone at mission control in Houston feeling? Quote the words that tell you. (AF2, AF3, 3 marks)

They were nervous, worried, tense, anxious, afraid — 1 mark
'You can slice the air with a razor'; 'eyes are glued to computer screens' — 1 mark
'There's no sound'; 'No one dares move' — 1 mark

3. When Neil Armstrong first backed out of the *Eagle* spacecraft and climbed down the ladder onto the Moon, what was he feeling? Which words tell you? (AF2,AF3, 4 marks)

Very nervous but very excited — 1 mark
'Desperately excited'; 'struggling to hide it' — 1 mark
'voice is electric with tension' — 1 mark
'every nerve is tingling' — 1 mark

4. List all the things the astronauts left behind them on the Moon. Do you think they should have left all these things? (AF2, AF3, 5 marks)

- Used equipment
- Footprints
- US flag
- Lots of litter
- They shouldn't have left them because they will always be there (no wind or rain to clear them away)
- They had to leave them because they were too heavy to take back; *Eagle* must be light to take off

5. Re-read the last part of the text, from 'The astronauts push the precious samples – 22 kg of moon rocks – into the *Eagle* …' to the end.

a Why does the writer use the word 'precious' to describe the samples of moon rocks? (AF5, 2 marks)

Reward simple comment, e.g. *They've taken a lot of effort to collect; They are the first ever samples from the moon; They don't want to damage them or lose any*

b Why does the writer say the Earth is like 'a small blue and white marble'? (AF5, 2 marks)

Reward simple comment, e.g. *It tells you the shape is round; The sea is blue and the clouds are white; The Earth has colour but the Moon doesn't; The Earth looks like a coloured marble.*

Make judgements about texts, supporting ideas with evidence

Secure developing reader

Assessment

Duration: 1 hour

Resources needed	Lesson aims	Framework Objectives
• Teacher's Guide page 73: starter activity on writer's effects • Student Book pages 52–53: extracts from science fiction stories • Teacher's Guide pages 74–77: Assessment Task 2 and answers	• to know how to scan for and locate relevant information in answer to specific questions • to be able to extract information from a text for a specific purpose • to be able to express an opinion about a text	Y7: R6, **R8** Y8: R4, **R5**
	Target areas • Target area 1: Finding and using textual reference • Target area 4: Using empathy to make judgements	**Assessment Focuses** AF2, AF3, AF4, AF5, AF6

Starter (15 minutes)

Display the prompt phrases from the previous lesson: 'When the writer says "......." I can see ...; The word "......" makes me feel ...; I like the part where it says "........." because ...; I think ...'

Remind students what AF5 for reading asks them to do: make comments about the writer's choice of words and their effect on the reader. Display the extract from *The War of the Worlds* on page 73 of the Teacher's Guide. Read it aloud, reminding students how to read ahead to the end of a sentence and how to pick out the main clauses. Emphasise how punctuation aids meaning.

Using the annotations to guide you, explain to students which words in the text you have highlighted and linked, and how you have used these to speculate about the story and the characters in it. Model how to use the prompt phrases to comment on the writer's effects, e.g. 'When the writer says "the Thing" it suggests that people on earth don't really know what the Martians are sending. It sounds like a dangerous weapon but we don't know for certain, which makes it more frightening.'

As a whole class, you could consolidate further by practising using the prompt phrases on display to make comments about the writer's effects in another extract, e.g. in *Exodus:* 'The words "trunk" and "roots" make me feel that the buildings in the new city are huge and solid, like very large trees, but growing out of the sea bed, not earth.'

Introduction (15 minutes)

Remind students of the learning objective: to be able to make judgements about texts, supporting ideas with evidence. Explain that in the next two lessons they will be working independently on an Assessment Task based on a science fiction story. Share ideas about the typical features of the science fiction genre, e.g. by drawing on films they have seen. Direct students to the short extracts from three science fiction stories (Student Book pages 52–53), the first of which they have just seen in the starter activity. In groups of four, they should read each extract aloud, paying attention to the punctuation, e.g. by reading sentences in turn. They should then use the response cards to help them comment on each extract in more detail. They could take one card each within the group, prepare answers to the prompts and then take it in turns to tell the others what they think. As a group, they can then decide answers to the questions: 'What is the main idea about the future in each extract? Which story would you most want to read and why?'

As a whole class, feed back some answers to these questions and to those on the response cards. Encourage speculation, based on clues in the texts.

Development (20 minutes)

Direct students to pages 54 and 55 of the Student Book, the longer extract from *Exodus* by Julie Bertagna. Show students how to skim-read the text by running a finger and their eyes down the centre of the text, looking for words either side of the central line. This should yield some of the key nouns that will help establish the text type and key events, e.g. *Mara, sky city, sea police, guards, identi-disk*

Make judgements about texts, supporting ideas with evidence

Secure developing reader

Assessment

Duration: 1 hour

and so on.

Give students Assessment Task 2 and read the instructions and questions with them to check that they understand what to do. They will answer some of the questions by highlighting the text itself, so will need individual copies (Teacher's Guide pages 74–75).

Students work independently to complete Assessment Task 2. Teacher to intervene only as needed. This should take them about 20 minutes.

Plenary (10 minutes)

Students complete Assessment Task 2.

If appropriate, individuals/pairs can use the answer sheets (pages 76–77 of the Teacher's Guide) to mark their own or each other's assessments and provide feedback. Alternatively, they can do this in the next lesson when they have also finished the second part of the Assessment Task.

Extension activity

Imagine you are exploring the sky city, as Mara does in the story. What might you see and do in this city of the future?

Secure developing reader

Starter activity: annotating a text to highlight writer's effects

Space
Shows us how far away Mars is from the earth, yet not far enough to keep the earth safe from attack.

Across the **gulf of space**, **minds that were vast and cool and unsympathetic**, regarded this earth with **envious eyes**, and slowly and surely the Martians drew their plans against us. And invisible to us because it was so remote and small, flying swiftly and steadily towards us across that incredible distance, drawing nearer every minute by so many thousands of miles, came **the Thing** they were sending us, **the Thing** that was to bring us so much **struggle** and **calamity** and **death** to the earth.

envious
They are jealous of humans on earth – perhaps conditions on their own planet have changed so they can't live there any more. They want the air and water that we have.

vast, cool, unsympathetic
These words suggest that the Martians are very cleve and also unemotional; they won't have a conscience about invading earth.

Thing
The way the word Things is repeated makes us wonder what it is – a missile of some kind, or a space ship, flying towards the earth? Repetition highlights its danger.

struggle, calamity, death
These linked words show us how much of a threat the Martians are; they will bring suffering and destruction to the earth.

Secure developing reader

Assessment Task 2: Mara steals a police uniform and slips into the city

Name ______________________________ Date ______________

The door of the lift capsule to the sky city is wide open. Workers from the early morning supply ship are surging through, sweaty and dirty and tired, along with a squad of sea police. Wearing the orange uniform, it's easy to merge in. As she approaches the lift capsule she almost stops. A single step more will take her across the threshold that separates the two worlds. In the end it's the crush of those behind rather then her own will that pushes her through the doorway into the large golden capsule.

The next thing Mara sees when she steps out of the lift capsule is a line of city guards. Heart pounding, she avoids eye contact and walks past… Mara's stomach lurches, and not just from nerves. She feels as if she is on a ship at sea – gently but unnervingly the city sways to the rhythm of the world's wind, as it is built to do.

'Hey, you! Over here!' a guard shouts and Mara forces herself not to turn around but to keep moving with the rest. Her instinct is right. It's someone else they want. Mara follows the crowd from the supply ship down a short corridor and waits her turn in the queue, trying to look at ease but concentrating fiercely on everything around her.

'To enter, please insert your identi-disk here,' announces a voice, over and over, at the head of the queue. Its owner is a blankly smiling young woman who stands at the head of the corridor at what must be the official doorway to New Mungo… With relief, Mara sees that she's only a lumen-being, crafted from light… The lumen girl points at the slit in the wall where Mara should insert an identi-disk.

'To enter, please insert your identi-disk here,' the lumen girl instructs.

Mara guesses and inserts one of the disks…

'Incorrect disk.'

The slot in the wall ejects the first disk. Mara doesn't dare look at the line of city guards and frantically, her fingers shaking, she inserts the second disk… The sliding door opens. Mara slips through, her heart beating painfully.

And is in! Amazed, she stands inside a long silver tunnel.

Secure developing reader

Before you read the whole text:

- Scan the story to find the following words and highlight them on the text: *lift capsule*, *sky city*, *sea police*, *city guards*, *identi-disk*, *lumen-being.*

As you read the whole text:

- Underline the words in the text that you weren't able to read straight away. Use the strategies you know to make sense of an unfamiliar word:
  - o sound it out
  - o look for patterns you know
  - o think what word would fit in the sentence
  - o use context clues to help you decide what the word could be.
- Now circle any words you still can't read.

After you've read the whole text:

- Check your understanding. Read the statements below and circle the correct answer:

The lift capsule moves slowly.	True	False	We aren't told
Mara doesn't look at the city guards.	True	False	We aren't told
Mara turns round when a guard shouts, 'Hey, you!'	True	False	We aren't told
The lumen-being speaks very loudly.	True	False	We aren't told
The lumen-being is not human but made out of light.	True	False	We aren't told
The identi-disks are made out of plastic.	True	False	We aren't told
The sky city is called New Mango.	True	False	We aren't told
The sky city is built to move gently in the wind.	True	False	We aren't told
The doorway opens when Mara inserts the first disk.	True	False	We aren't told

- Use letters (A–A, B–B, etc.) to match together these main clauses and subordinate clauses and make the same sentences that the writer uses. Check back in the text to see if you have made the right choices.

Frantically, her fingers shaking,	her heart beating painfully.
Mara slips through,	she inserts the second disk.
Heart pounding,	it's easy to merge in.
Wearing the orange uniform,	she avoids eye contact and walks past.

- Now number the sentences 1–4 to show the order in which they appear in the story.
- Complete the table below by writing in evidence from the text to show how Mara feels at key points in the story.

What Mara feels	**Evidence that shows her feelings**
When she first steps out of the lift capsule and sees the city guards, Mara feels very frightened and nervous.	1. 'heart pounding' 2.
When she inserts the second disk and then goes through the sliding door, Mara again feels very frightened and nervous.	1. 2.

Secure developing reader

Assessment Task 2: answers

This activity is testing students' ability to skim and scan independently and to locate specific information.

Before you read the whole text:

- Scan the story to find the following words and highlight them on the text: *lift capsule*, *sky city*, *sea police*, *city guards*, *identi-disk*, *lumen-being.*

This activity is testing students' ability to use a range of strategies independently to make sense of unfamiliar words, and their ability to self-correct when meaning doesn't make sense. (AF1)

As you read the whole text:

- Underline the words in the text that you weren't able to read straight away. Use the strategies you know to make sense of an unfamiliar word:
  - o sound it out
  - o look for patterns you know
  - o think what word would fit in the sentence
  - o use context clues to help you decide what the word could be.
- Now circle any words you still can't read.

This question is testing students' ability to retrieve simple facts from the text and to use inference and deduction (AF2, AF3)

After you've read the whole text:

- Check your understanding. Read the statements below and circle the correct answer:

The lift capsule moves slowly.	True	<u>False</u>	We aren't told
Mara doesn't look at the city guards.	<u>True</u>	False	We aren't told
Mara turns round when a guard shouts, 'Hey, you!'	True	<u>False</u>	We aren't told
The lumen-being speaks very loudly.	True	False	<u>We aren't told</u>
The lumen-being is not human but made out of light.	<u>True</u>	False	We aren't told
The identi-disks are made out of plastic.	True	False	<u>We aren't told</u>
The sky city is called New Mango.	True	<u>False</u>	We aren't told
The sky city is built to move gently in the wind.	<u>True</u>	False	We aren't told
The doorway opens when Mara inserts the first disk.	True	<u>False</u>	We aren't told

This question is testing students' ability to look at the structure of the whole text, read closely and sequence information (AF4)

- Use letters (A–A, B–B, etc.) to match together these main clauses and subordinate clauses and make the same sentences that the writer uses. Check back in the text to see if you have made the right choices.

Frantically, her fingers shaking,	**A**	**3**	her heart beating painfully.	**B**
Mara slips through,	**B**	**4**	she inserts the second disk.	**A**
Heart pounding,	**C**	**2**	it's easy to merge in.	**D**
Wearing the orange uniform,	**D**	**1**	she avoids eye contact and walks past.	**C**

- Now number the sentences 1–4 to show the order in which they appear in the story.

Secure developing reader

This question is testing students' ability to understand and select relevant evidence from the text (AF2)

- Complete the table below by writing in evidence from the text to show how Mara feels at key points in the story.

What Mara feels	Evidence that shows her feelings
When she first steps out of the lift capsule and sees the city guards, Mara feels very frightened and nervous.	1. 'heart pounding' 2. 'Mara's stomach lurches'/ 'she avoids eye contact'
When she inserts the second disk and then goes through the sliding door, Mara again feels very frightened and nervous.	1. 'frantically'/ 'her fingers shaking' 2. 'her heart beating painfully'

Lesson Plan 3 of 3

Make judgements about texts, supporting ideas with evidence

Secure developing reader

Assessment

Duration: 1 hour

Resources needed	Lesson aims	Assessment Focuses
• Student Book pages 54–55: extract from *Exodus* • Teacher's Guide pages 79–83: Assessment Task 3 and answers • Teacher's Guide page 85: Assessment grid	• to know how to scan for and locate relevant information in answer to specific questions • to be able to extract information from a text for a specific purpose • to be able to express an opinion about a text **Target areas** • Target area 1: Finding and using textual reference • Target area 4: Using empathy to make judgements	AF2, AF3, AF5, AF6

Starter (15 minutes)

Direct students to the extract from *Exodus* in the Student Book and ask them to scan the whole text for all the words they can find that suggest the story is science fiction, set in an imaginary future world. Stress that they are looking for nouns that 'name' objects and people in this future world, e.g. *lift capsule*, *sky city*, *sea police*, *identi-disk*, *lumen-being*, *Zoominium*, *Looking Pond*. Together, draw up a glossary that will explain what these things are, looking in the text to help and filling out details by speculating and imagining.

Introduction (15 minutes)

Give students individual copies of Assessment Task 3. Read the instructions and questions together to clarify understanding of what they have to do. Stress that some of the questions relate to the whole extract from *Exodus*. They can either refer to this in the Student Book pages 54–55, or you could re-issue Assessment Task 2.

Students work independently to complete Assessment Task 3. The teacher can work with a guided group of weaker students to observe and assist in completion of the task, or work with individuals, e.g. to listen to them read the extract whilst taking a running record (see introduction to Teacher's Guide page xii).

Development (20 minutes)

Students complete work on Assessment Task 3.

Plenary (10 minutes)

Complete self-assessment star rating using the criteria on page 55 of the Student Book or page 85 in Teacher's Guide.

Some answers can be marked by students, using pages 82–3 of the Teacher's Guide.

Extension activity

Reflect on your achievements in this assessment cycle and set yourself a target for improving your reading skills.

Secure developing reader

Assessment Task 3: Mara explores the sky city to find out how things work

Name ______________________________ Date ______________

All she needs to do is to look as if she has lived in a sky city all her life – not easy when at every step there are such wonders that all she wants to do is stop and stare. Mara explores the city centre, trying to get her bearings.

Zoominium, says a sign above one large window. Mara peers through and sees what looks like a deep pool, but instead of water, people wheel and tumble through cascades of colour. Mara feels overwhelmed by so much glare, noise and movement, and by so many people.

But New Mungo is beautiful. Its long silver tunnels gleam and its arcades are vast airy places that look as if they, like the population of lumens, are crafted purely from light. The citizens are beautiful too…a world full of brilliant beings, human angels.

A happy crowd of boys and girls near her own age zip past on skates. So that's the secret of their speed and power! Mara stares enviously at their strong bodies, bright smiles and smooth skins. She stops at a humpbacked bridge that sits under a crystal sky and leans upon the bridge wall to look into the still mirror of a pond. Mara relaxes into the gentle wind-sway of the city as she watches the fish swimming round the Looking Pond and listens to the birdsong in the tree beside the bridge. A radiant sunset spreads across the screen of water, deepening and darkening until the pond is midnight black and full of star fire.

It would be so easy to forget the rest of the world, so tempting to slip inside this magic spell and ignore what lies outside.

Now the horror of the boat camp on the other side of the wall rushes upon her, along with the memory of her lost family. She looks at the pond with clear eyes. The fish are fake and swim in endless electronic circles. The tree and its bird, the crystal sky and sunset, are all fake too. It's a false enchantment.

Now Mara is bitter, right to the brim. It gives her the burst of energy she needs. A cool, clear head and courage. One step at a time. The next step is to find food and somewhere to stay.

Assessment Lesson 3

Secure developing reader

Before you read the whole text:

- Scan the story to find the parts that describe what Mara does and how she feels. Highlight them on the text:
  - o Mara explores the city centre
  - o Mara feels overwhelmed
  - o Mara stops at a humpbacked bridge
  - o she watches the fish swimming
  - o the horror of the boat camp … rushes upon her
  - o Now Mara is bitter

As you read the whole text:

- Underline the words in the text that you weren't able to read straight away. Use the strategies you know to make sense of an unfamiliar word:
  - o sound it out
  - o look for patterns you know
  - o think what word would fit in the sentence
  - o use context clues to help you decide what the word could be.
- Now circle any words you still can't read.

After you've read the whole text:

- Read the paragraph that starts 'Zoominium, says a sign above one large window.' Write down any two details that tell you what a *zoominium* is:

____

____

- What makes Mara feel 'overwhelmed'. Write down any **two** details.

____

____

Secure developing reader

- The writer says, 'New Mungo is beautiful'. Highlight the words the writer uses to show how beautiful the city is:

  Its long silver tunnels gleam and its arcades are vast airy places that look as if they, like the population of lumens, are crafted purely from light. The citizens are beautiful too…a world full of brilliant beings, human angels…

- The writer says, 'A happy crowd of boys and girls near her own age *zip* past on skates.' Circle two other words in this list that are closest in meaning to *zip*.

  crawl   zoom   hop   fly   stagger   plod

- When Mara peers into the Looking Pond more closely, she sees that:

  'The fish are fake and swim in endless electronic circles. The tree and its bird, the crystal sky and sunset, are all fake too. It's a false enchantment.'

  - o circle the word above that means the same as fake.
  - o circle the word from this list that is closest in meaning to enchantment: pain   magic   wish

- Think about both parts of the story. Based on evidence in the text, rate the statements below as follows:

  - o ✓ I agree with this statement
  - o × I do not agree with this statement
  - o ? I'm not sure about this statement

  Mara thinks the sky city is boring.

  Mara thinks the sky city is beautiful.

  Mara forgets all about the world outside the sky city.

  Mara does not want to be noticed by the city guards.

  Mara screams when she inserts the wrong identi-disk.

  Mara is brave.

  Mara is angry when she finds out the Looking Pond is fake and unreal.

  Mara wishes she could live in the sky city forever.

- Based on this extract, would you want to read more of this story? Give at least two reasons for your answer.

  ____

  ____

Secure developing reader

Assessment Task 3: answers

This activity is testing students' ability to skim and scan independently and to locate specific information. (AF2)

Before you read the whole text:

- Scan the story to find the parts that describe what Mara does and how she feels. Highlight them on the text:
  - o Mara explores the city centre
  - o Mara feels overwhelmed
  - o Mara stops at a humpbacked bridge
  - o she watches the fish swimming
  - o the horror of the boat camp … rushes upon her
  - o Now Mara is bitter

This activity is testing students' ability to use a range of strategies independently to make sense of unfamiliar words, and their ability to self-correct when meaning doesn't make sense. (AF1)

As you read the whole text:

- Underline the words in the text that you weren't able to read straight away. Use the strategies you know to make sense of an unfamiliar word:
  - o sound it out
  - o look for patterns you know
  - o think what word would fit in the sentence
  - o use context clues to help you decide what the word could be.
- Now circle any words you still can't read.

These questions are testing students' ability to select and understand information in the text (AF2)

After you've read the whole text:

- Read the paragraph that starts 'Zoominium, says a sign above one large window.' Write down any two details that tell you what a *zoominium* is:

  Students can use own words or direct quotes; any two from: looks like a deep pool; a waterfall/cascade of colour/where people play/wheel and tumble (AF2)

- What makes Mara feel 'overwhelmed'. Write down any **two** details.

  Students can use own words or direct quotes; any two from: the glare/bright lights; the noise; the movement; so many people (AF2)

Secure developing reader

These questions are testing students' understanding of writer's choice of words for effect (AF5)

- The writer says, 'New Mungo is beautiful'. Highlight the words the writer uses to show how beautiful the city is:

  Its long <u>silver tunnels gleam</u> and its arcades are <u>vast airy</u> places that look as if they, like the population of lumens, are <u>crafted purely from light</u>. The citizens are beautiful too…a world full of <u>brilliant</u> beings, human <u>angels</u>…

- The writer says, 'A happy crowd of boys and girls near her own age *zip* past on skates.' Circle two other words in this list that are closest in meaning to *zip*.

  crawl <u>zoom</u> hop <u>fly</u> stagger plod

- When Mara peers into the Looking Pond more closely, she sees that:

  'The fish are fake and swim in endless electronic circles. The tree and its bird, the crystal sky and sunset, are all fake too. It's a <u>false</u> enchantment.'

  - circle the word above that means the same as fake.
  - circle the word from this list that is closest in meaning to enchantment: pain <u>magic</u> wish

These questions are testing students' ability to think about the writer's purposes and to make judgements based on evidence (AF6)

- Think about both parts of the story. Based on evidence in the text, rate the statements below as follows:
  - ✓ I agree with this statement
  - × I do not agree with this statement
  - ? I'm not sure about this statement

  Most likely answers:

Mara thinks the sky city is boring.	×
Mara thinks the sky city is beautiful.	✓
Mara forgets all about the world outside the sky city.	×
Mara does not want to be noticed by the city guards.	✓
Mara screams when she inserts the wrong identi-disk.	×
Mara is brave.	✓
Mara is angry when she finds out the Looking Pond is fake and unreal.	✓
Mara wishes she could live in the sky city for ever.	×

- Based on this extract, would you want to read more of this story? Give at least two reasons for your answer.

  Look for simple comments supported by some evidence that is based on response to the text e.g. 'I like the way the city is described'; 'I want to find out what the food is like.'

Secure developing reader

Name ____________________ Date ____________

Assessment Focuses for Reading	If I'm Level 2, I can ...	If I'm Level 3, I can ...
AF2 Understand, describe, select or retrieve information, events and ideas from texts and use quotation and reference to text	• use different strategies to read unfamiliar words, e.g. phonic knowledge, grammar and context clues. • scan text to locate specific details. • identify and select the main ideas in texts. • usually notice when something I read doesn't make sense and go back and correct it. • read ahead to make sense of the whole sentence.	• use a range of reading strategies independently to tackle unfamiliar words. • identify straightforward and more obvious points in texts, although I sometimes misunderstand. • quote from, or refer to, the text to back up my points, although I don't always choose relevant evidence.
AF3 Deduce, infer or interpret information, events or ideas from texts	• understand straightforward factual information in texts. • understand main ideas in texts. • recount main events or facts with some help. • express an opinion or preference. • find some details in the text in answer to specific questions.	• understand factual information and literal meanings in texts. • try to read between the lines to find deeper meanings. • make straightforward comments when talking about a text. • give a personal view about a text. • quote some details from the text or refer to information in it that supports my ideas.
AF4 Identify and comment on the structure and organisation of texts, including grammatical and presentational features at word and sentence level	• comment on some obvious features of the way information is presented, e.g. use of pictures, headlines and titles and give simple reasons for their use. • locate topic sentences. • see how the main ideas are sequenced in a text.	• identify and comment on some straightforward features of presentation, e.g. headings or illustrations, subheadings • identify some of the ways in which the text is organised and structured, e.g. the order in which points are made; how the text begins and ends.
AF5 explain and comment on writers' use of language, including grammatical and literary features at word and sentence level	• locate specific words and phrases in answer to questions. • read aloud with expression to show that I've understood the writer's intentions.	• identify a few straightforward features of the writer's use of language, although I might not add a comment about them, e.g. 'The writer uses lots of adjectives.'
AF6 Identify and comment on writers' purposes and viewpoints, and the overall effect of the text on the reader.	• understand and comment on some simple features of the text such as the plot, characters or setting • identify the main purpose of the text and give simple reasons • express an opinion or preference about events and actions.	• identify and comment on the main purpose of the text and the writer's viewpoint, e.g. 'the writer doesn't like violence'. • give a straightforward personal response to the text. • express opinions and state preferences.

Secure developing reader

Assessment Tasks: Space and science fiction

Name ______________________ Date __________

You have been learning:

- to make judgements about texts, supporting ideas with evidence.

Give yourself a 1–3 star rating for each of the skills listed below. 3 stars = I can do this easily; 2 stars = I can do this with some help; 1 star = I need a lot of help with this.

Your teacher will also assess you ✓ = you can do this independently; ? = you need some help with this; X = you still need a lot of help with this.

Assessment criteria	Your assessment rating	Teacher assessment
• identify and understand the main ideas in texts		
• read a text closely and empathise with what the characters are feeling and thinking		
• find some details in the text in answer to specific questions		
• quote from, or refer to the text, to support my ideas with evidence		
• give my opinion about events, ideas or characters		

My reading target is ....

Lesson Plan 1 of 3

Using reading strategies to infer and deduce meaning in fiction texts

Competent reader

Cycle A

Duration: 1 hour

Resources needed	Lesson aims	Assessment Focuses
• Student Book pages 56–59: making deductions • CD-ROM Cycle A (Competent reader) resource sheet 1.1: cut-up cards • CD-ROM Cycle A (Competent reader) resource sheets 1.2 and 1.3: making a deduction	• to be able to select relevant information in a text • to be able to link details in a text in order to make a deduction **Target areas** • Target area 1: Reading between the lines	AF2, AF3

Starter (15 minutes)

Explain to the students how important it is to be able to find strong information from an image or text to back up things we say about that image or text. As a class, consider the first zoomed in detail on page 56 of the Student Book and read the statement about that image. Model the selection of information to support the statement, identifying relevant *literal/explicit* information from the image to support the statement. Ask the class: 'How do I know that this information is relevant?' Model the use of 'Be relevant!' aloud with the class. In pairs, students read the statement for the second zoomed in detail. Hand out cards for image 2 (resource sheet 1.1). In pairs, students discuss which pieces of evidence from the picture are relevant to the statement, using the process outlined in 'Be relevant!'

Introduction (15 minutes)

Students form pairs where student A is the selector and student B is the tester of relevance. Using the zoomed in detail and statement 3, student A must find between three and five pieces of information/evidence from the image to support the statement and student B must decide whether that evidence is 'relevant', using the 'Be relevant!' process.

Explain to the class that they are getting better at finding relevant pieces of information, and that the next step is to put those pieces of evidence together to form a bigger picture. Explain that we call this process deducing, or making a deduction. Ask: 'What can I work out about the situation in this picture by making links between the smaller parts?' Individuals have 90 seconds to think about possible links between the four close-up pictures. In pairs, students share their links and deductions to build confidence. As a class, discuss the possible links between the three close-up pictures and the possible links between the statements about the pictures. Model a possible answer, showing how details from the close-ups can be added up to help make a deduction to answer the question. Express the process like a sum, written on the board: _____ from picture A + ____ from image B = __deduction__. Encourage the students to have a go at making deductions using the sum format.

Development (20 minutes)

Display on a projector the text on resource sheet 1.2. Read the text as a class, then give individual students 2 minutes to re-read the text to themselves on pages 58–59 of the Student Book, identifying unfamiliar words and applying their reading strategies for tackling them. Allow a further minute to share with a partner the words that they found difficult to read, explaining the strategies they used to tackle them. Explain to the students that they are now going to combine the two reading skills they have been practising in this lesson: they are going to select relevant information from the text and try to make links between that information so that they can make a deduction. In pairs, students read the statements surrounding the text on pages 58–59 of the Student Book and take turns at finding information from the text to support the image, checking the relevance of the information found using the 'Be relevant!' guidelines on page 56 of the Student Book. Signal to the students when you want them to start making deductions using the blank sum beneath the image, speaking aloud their deductions.

Plenary (10 minutes)

As a class, tackle the big questions: What *is* 'deduction'? What do we *do in our minds* when we make a deduction? Focus attention on the images on resource sheet 1.3. **In pairs,** students discuss how the

Using reading strategies to infer and deduce meaning in fiction texts

Competent reader

Cycle A

Duration: 1 hour

images relate to the process of making links between information from a text and adding up bits of information to make a deduction. They need to consider: *which of these images will be useful in helping me to remember what to do to make a deduction and why?* Share responses as a class.

Lesson Plan 2 of 3

Using reading strategies to infer and deduce meaning in fiction texts

Competent reader

Cycle A

Duration: 1 hour

Resources needed	Lesson aims	Assessment Focuses
• Student Book pages 60–61: 'The iceberg of meaning' • Student Book pages 62–63: 'What does it mean?' • CD-ROM Cycle A (Competent reader) resource sheet 2.1: cut-up cards • CD-ROM Cycle A (Competent Reader) resource sheet 2.2: iceberg image	• to understand that some meanings are literal and some meanings are non-literal • to be able to link details in a text in order to make a deduction • to be able to select relevant information from a text **Target areas** • Target area 1: Reading between the lines	AF2, AF3

Starter (15 minutes)

Ask the class: 'What do you think of when you see this image of an iceberg? What does the word *iceberg* link with in your mind?' Allow the students one minute's thinking time in pairs to develop confidence. Take feedback as a class brainstorm, forming a list on the board; the rule is that no one can comment on any of the suggestions made by class members as the suggestions are being made. Then, as a class, question any of the listed suggestions to make sure that their meaning is clarified.

Turn to pages 60–61 of the Student Book. With the class, read the definitions of literal and non-literal meaning. Explain that you are going to read aloud some of the responses that other people have made with icebergs. Some will be surface level, literal, factual meanings, but other responses will be deeper, non-literal meanings that require us to think more deeply. Read the first response aloud: 'Icebergs are made of frozen water,' and talk about your reasons for placing it above the waterline. Read out the rest of the responses, allowing pairs of students 20 seconds after each one to decide *where* they think it belongs on the iceberg of meaning. Insist that they verbalise their reasons.

1 Some icebergs are very big.
2 Icebergs are slowly melting.
3 Looking at an iceberg makes me feel lonely.
4 Icebergs are a ship's enemies!
5 Icebergs are pieces of broken glacier.
6 Icebergs are like beautiful jewels.
7 Icebergs move.
8 Icebergs make me feel small.

Tie up this session by asking the students to explain to their partner, in their own words, how we can tell the difference between literal (surface) and non-literal (beneath the surface) information.

Introduction (15 minutes)

Turn to page 62 of the Student Book and allow students one minute to 'read' the image. As a class, read the statements around the image. Explain that some of the statements have literal meanings and some have non-literal meanings. Model the thought process involved in deciding whether the first statement is literal or non-literal and therefore where it would be placed on the iceberg of meaning. Individually, students continue to read through the statements and decide whether they are literal or non-literal and where they should be placed on the iceberg of meaning.

Give further guidance to students who have found this difficult, by organising a guided group and re-running through some of the statements, asking for their responses and their reasoning. Students who are comfortable with the distinction could extend their understanding by formulating a literal and a non-literal statement of their own about the picture, ready to share later on. Tie up this session by asking the students to explain to their partner, in their own words, how we can tell the difference between statements that draw on literal meaning from a text and statements that draw on non-literal meaning from a text.

Development (20 minutes)

Lesson Plan 2 of 3

Using reading strategies to infer and deduce meaning in fiction texts

Competent reader

Cycle A

Duration: 1 hour

Give pairs of students copies of resource sheet 2.1, cut up into its different parts, one set of cards per pair. Explain that the cards show different parts of a text that they will read later in the lesson. Some of these pieces of information **tell** us that the person in the story is afraid – these bits of information are literal. Some of the pieces of information **suggest** that the person is afraid – these pieces of information are non-literal and we are required to read beneath the waterline. Using resource sheet 2.2 or the image of the iceberg on pages 60–61 of the Student Book, pairs of students sort the cards, placing them above (literal) or below (non-literal) the waterline.

Next, focus attention on the text on page 63 of the Student Book. Students read the text on their own and spend one minute thinking about their responses to it. Give pairs of students a further minute to share some of their initial responses to the text, to build confidence. Take the first statement from around the outside of the text on page 63. Model the thought processes involved in deciding whether this statement draws on literal or non-literal meaning by returning to details in the text and how to decide where the statement would be placed on the iceberg of meaning. Uncover the remaining responses for pairs of students to work through together, verbalising their thoughts and the decisions they are making about the statements and the text.

Plenary (10 minutes)

Ask the students to cast their minds back to the previous lesson; ask: 'What do we do when we make a deduction?' Give one minute's thinking time and then allow the students to talk about their ideas with a partner. Establish a definition for 'deduction' and remind the students of the sum format used in the previous lesson. Draw attention to the question beneath the text and allow three minutes to discuss links between the relevant details in the text. Set a challenge: can pairs of students use the sum format to make a deduction in answer to the question? The only rule is that they try to link one literal and one non-literal detail from the text to make their deduction.

Lesson Plan 3 of 3

Using reading strategies to infer and deduce meaning in fiction texts

Competent reader

Cycle A

Duration: 1 hour

Resources needed	Lesson aims	Assessment Focuses
• Student Book pages 64–65: 'Between the lines' • CD-ROM Cycle A (Competent reader) resource sheet 3.1: cut-up cards	• to understand that some meanings are literal and some meanings are non-literal • to be able to use a range of reading strategies to access meaning • to be able to draw conclusions about meaning **Target areas** • Target area 1: Reading between the lines	AF2, AF3

Starter (15 minutes)

Give pairs of students 30 seconds to remember what we do when we make a deduction. Explain that this lesson we are going to take our deductions one step further: we are going to learn how to draw a conclusion. Ask the pairs to imagine that they are tracking a wild animal. They don't know what type of animal it is; they don't know how far ahead of them it is. Hand out cut-up cards from resource sheet 3.1. Students discuss what the details tell them about the animal. After two minutes, ask the students to make links between the details and begin to make deductions. How many deductions can they make about the animal? They should come up to the board and clearly record one of their deductions in the sum format modelled in lesson one. Stop the class and read the deductions together. If any of the deductions contradict one another, ask the writers of those deductions to explain their thinking and then ask the class if they can accept one, the other or both of the deductions. Explain to the students that they are now going to draw a conclusion. To do this, they need to step back and look at all the deductions. Can they see the 'big picture'? Can they put together some of the deductions and draw a big conclusion about the animal? Model the linking of deductions to form a conclusion, using: 'We deduced that ... and … so I conclude that …' Encourage the students to have a go.

Introduction (15 minutes)

Focus attention on the image on pages 64–65 of the Student Book. Tell the students that you want them to read the picture on a literal level to begin with. Give the students one minute to look at and think about the image before modelling the process of verbalising a literal detail, e.g. 'There are two boys in this picture.' Once you have verbalised the literal detail, ask one of the students to find one. Continue to verbalise details and 'pass' the turn around the room until the picture is exhausted.

Now organise the students into pairs. Explain that you want them to use one of their active reading strategies to read beneath the surface of the image. Give them four minutes to come up with questions that will get beneath the surface of the image and unlock the non-literal meanings: they should record each of their questions on a separate strip of paper. Join the pairs into groups of four. Students turn to page 60–61 of the Student Book and share their questions, deciding where the questions should go on the 'iceberg of meaning'. You could model this process by taking one of the student's questions and explaining where you will place it and why.

Development (20 minutes)

Use the prompt cards from Assessment lesson 1 (Teacher's Guide page 112) to remind the students of the active reading strategies they learnt to use in previous lessons. Give the students one minute to remind themselves what each strategy means and what they 'do' when they read in each of these ways. Look at the fragments of text around the image on pages 64–65. These fragments relate to the image in some way. Model the process of using at least two of the active reading strategies to make sense of a fragment and then relate the fragment to the image, thinking each stage out loud. Tell the students that to be successful in this activity they need to speak all of their thoughts out loud. Pairs of students take it in turns to read, make sense of and 'place' the fragments. Take feedback by asking for the class to volunteer the names of those who did particularly well in speaking their thoughts aloud.

Using reading strategies to infer and deduce meaning in fiction texts

Competent reader

Cycle A

Duration: 1 hour

Plenary (10 minutes)
Model the process of making a deduction, using the sum format, linking two details, one from the text and one from the image. Use the following stems: • From this detail I deduced … and from this detail I deduced • So I conclude … In pairs, students have a go at drawing a conclusion

Choosing appropriate reading strategies

Competent reader

Cycle B

Duration: 1 hour

Resources needed	Lesson aims	Assessment Focuses
• Student Book pages 66–67: 'Skimming for meaning' • CD-ROM Cycle B (Competent reader) resource sheet 1.1 (4 pages): images • CD-ROM Cycle B (Competent reader) resource sheet 1.2: copies of prompt card • CD-ROM Cycle B (Competent reader) resource sheet 1.3: copies of topic sentence strips • CD-ROM Cycle B (Competent reader) resource sheet 1.4 on CD-ROM: OHT of text for modelling skimming	• to know how to skim a text for its general meaning • to be able to put information from a text into own words **Target areas** • Target area 2: Using a range of reading strategies	AF2

Starter (15 minutes)

Introduce the word 'skim': where have the students heard this word before? Give one minute's thinking time and then let the students share their thoughts with a partner before gathering their responses. Explain that skimming is also a way of reading: when we skim a text we glance quickly through it to get a sense of what it is about. Explain that when we skim, we are not interested in the detail of the text; instead we want to get a sense of the main points. Using the image on pages 66–67 of the Student Book, model the process of skimming the image, speaking aloud what you do with your eyes and mind as you skim. Finish the modelling with: 'So, as I skimmed I noticed … and I think that this image is about …' After modelling, point out to the class that you have not been interested in the detail of the picture. In pairs, students read through the statements surrounding the image and discuss whether they are details or whether they are main points about the image. Recap on skimming, using the bullet points on page 66 of the Student Book.

Introduction (15 minutes)

Organise the students into teams of four. Give one prompt card (resource sheet 1.2) to each group. Explain that, one at a time, a member of each team will visit the teacher's desk and have 20 seconds to skim an image they will be shown (resource sheet 1.4). During these 20 seconds they must skim for the main points of meaning in the image before returning to their team to share the skimmed meaning and explain what they think the picture is about. They should use the prompt card to help them if they get stuck. The role of the group members is to listen and then repeat the overall statement, 'So, this is an image about …' at the end of the explanation.

Tell the class that skimming a written text requires similar skills. Explain what a topic sentence is: it acts as a signpost to the reader; it comes at the beginning of a paragraph; it gives us an idea of what that paragraph is going to be 'about'. Repeat your explanation once, then give the students an opportunity to explain it in their own words to three other students in the room, beginning: 'A topic sentence is …'

Organise the students into pairs. Explain that you are going to give them the topic sentences of a short text and hand out the first set of topic sentence strips from resource sheet 1.3. Pairs of students read the topic sentences and try to work out what the text is likely to be 'about'. Can they put the topic sentences in an order? Can they explain what they think the text is going to be 'about' in a single sentence? Pairs practise verbalising what they think the text will be about, then leave their chairs to share with other pairs in the room. Take some of these summaries from the class and comment on the similarities and differences between them.

Development (20 minutes)

Working independently, students repeat the process of making links between topic sentences using the

Choosing appropriate reading strategies

Cycle B

Duration: 1 hour

second set of Teacher's Guide strips. Make time for the students to repeatedly verbalise their summary of the text, to build their confidence. Ask them to remind themselves: '*Where* are topic sentences in a text?' Using resource sheet 1.4, model the skimming of the text by identifying and reading the topic sentences. Speak aloud the thought process involved in making a link between these sentences and making an overall statement about the text.

Ask the class to help you to test the summary you have made based on your skimming, by reading the whole text aloud together and stopping briefly after each paragraph to discuss whether the detail supports the summary. Using the bullet-pointed success criteria on page 66 of the Student Book, pairs of students remind themselves of the process of skimming a text and talk about which aspects of it they find most difficult.

Plenary (10 minutes)

Individually, students use the text on page 67 of the Student Book to test their skimming skills, speaking aloud as they skim. In pairs, they share their 'summary' of the text and discuss how well they personally did, using the numbered success criteria on page 67 of the Student Book to guide them. They should set a target for the next time they skim.

Lesson Plan 2 of 3

Choosing appropriate reading strategies

Competent reader

Cycle B

Duration: 1 hour

Resources needed	Lesson aims	Assessment Focuses
• Student Book pages 68–69: 'What is this question asking me?' • CD-ROM Cycle B (Competent reader) resource sheet 2.1: questions for discussion	• to be able to select information relevant to a question or task • to know how to skim a text for its general meaning **Target areas** • Target area 3: Finding the main ideas in a text and supporting them with evidence	AF2

Starter (15 minutes)

Point out to the students that sometimes the questions we are asked about texts are difficult to understand. Sometimes, we have to work hard to read the question itself so that we understand what we are being asked. Turn to pages 68–69 of the Student Book. Explain to the students that the questions on page 69 relate to the story on the page. Take the first question, write it on the board and model aloud the thought processes involved in reading the question and deciding what it is asking, annotating the question: 'It is asking "when?", so we are looking for a time'. This might be written as a number or it could be written in words. However, we are not just looking for any time – we want to know when Sasha arrived home. Finish the process by underlining the **key words** in the question, explaining that you are doing this so that if you lose track of your thoughts, you can glance back at the question and quickly remind yourself of the most important words of the question. As a class, take the second question and repeat the process, this time with the students suggesting and the teacher annotating. Hand out the rest of the questions (resource sheet 2.1). Pairs of students should continue this process, speaking their thoughts aloud and supporting one another's decisions.

Introduction (15 minutes)

Turn to the example question and images on page 68 of the Student Book. Explain to the students that they have just learnt how to read a question carefully. Now they are going to add another step to their skills: selecting evidence from a text which is relevant to the question they are being asked. Point out the question with its boxed key words and use the annotations to clarify thinking about what the question is asking. As a class, use the images with the corresponding question to discuss which details in the image are relevant to the question: 'Who is wearing the most unusual clothes?' Following the steps made clear in the Student Book, students should work right through the process from tackling the question to identifying relevant details in the image.

Development (20 minutes)

Explain to the students that before the end of the lesson they are going to read a text and they are going to answer the questions they looked at earlier in the lesson. Give individual students 30 seconds' thinking time to remember: 'What is a topic sentence?' Pair and share to clarify before defining as a class. Turn again to page 69 of the Student Book and model the process of using the steps of taking a question and scanning the topic sentences to decide which part of the text to go to for answers. In pairs, students should take turns, with A taking one of the other questions and following the steps, while B listens to them, making sure they are following the steps correctly and offering support if A gets stuck. Allow a minute for the students to give each other feedback: What did they do well? Which part of the process do they need to work on? Next, take one of the questions and model the process of scanning through the whole paragraph for an answer to the question, checking the answer with the question before committing yourself. Individual students should choose a different question; decide on the key paragraph to go to and scan the paragraph for the answer, using the 'I can' statements in the Student Book to guide them. They should then share this answer with a partner, explaining **how** they got it.

Plenary (10 minutes)

Remind the students of an important skill they learnt in the last lesson: being able to skim a text and

Choosing appropriate reading strategies

Cycle B

Duration: 1 hour

explain its overall gist. Re-read the topic sentences of this lesson's short story. If the students were asked to summarise or explain the gist of this story in one sentence, what would they say? Give them the stem 'This story is about ...' Allow pairs of students 90 seconds to discuss how they would complete this sentence. Join pairs into groups of four to share their ideas. Which of the summaries do they like the most? Present these to the class and talk about **how** they came to these summaries.

Lesson Plan 3 of 3

Choosing appropriate reading strategies

Competent reader

Cycle B

Duration: 1 hour

Resources needed	Lesson aims	Assessment Focuses
• Student Book pages 70–71: 'Scanning a text for information' • CD-ROM Cycle B (Competent reader) resource sheet 3.1: cut up cards	• to be able to select information relevant to a question or task • to know how to skim a text for its general meaning **Target areas** • Target area 3: Finding the main ideas in a text and supporting them with evidence	AF2

Starter (15 minutes)

Remind students of the reading skill they have been practising: skimming. Allow one minute for students to remind themselves what we do when we 'skim' a text and *why* we might choose to do this. Feedback to clarify and check that they understand the process.

Introduce a new reading skill: scanning. Where have the students heard the word *scan* before? Share some of their responses as a class. Make sure that they are clear about the differences between skimming and scanning.

Introduce the image on page 70 of the Student Book. First, to recap, model the process of skimming the text, speaking aloud your thought processes to find out what the text is about. Next, draw the students' attention to the success criteria for scanning beneath the image in the Student Book; students should use these criteria to assess you as you model.

Now model the process of scanning the image for information relating to the statement. Allow the students to give you feedback and set a target for you.

Introduction (15 minutes)

Organise the students into pairs: A and B. Hand out the statement cards on resource sheet 3.1, one set per pair. Without looking at them, students spread them out face down on the table. Explain that each card has a statement about the image on page 70 of the student book. Student A chooses a card, reads the statement and, using a finger, scans the image for details that are relevant to the statement. Student B's role is to watch closely and listen to A's thinking. If A falls silent, B should say: 'Speak your thoughts aloud!' A and B then swap roles. After each scan, the pair should assess how well the scanner did, using the success criteria, setting a target for the next time they scan.

Explain to the students that when scanning a written text we must be clear about what we are being asked to look for and what this information might look like in the text. Tell the students that they are going to scan a written text for information relevant to a series of statements. Using resource sheet 3.1 and using just the first statement to begin with, speak aloud the thought processes of deciding what kind of information to look for in the text, e.g. information related to time, so numbers or time words. In pairs, students discuss the rest of the statements and the kind of information they would need to scan for in the text for each one. Take feedback and clarify.

Development (25 minutes)

Turn to the text on page 71 of the Student Book. Explain that you want to get the gist of this text by skimming its meaning, before looking at it in any detail. Remind the students that in the past they have learned to skim by reading the first sentence of each paragraph. Explain that this time you are going to skim the first few words of each sentence. Model aloud the process of skimming the first few words of each sentence in the first paragraph. At the end of the paragraph make some links and summarise what you have learned by skimming. In pairs, the students follow by extending the skimming to the second paragraph. Take feedback of their summaries. Organise the students into new pairs and label the students A and B. Give them one minute to remind themselves how to skim and then scan the text, putting the gist of the text into their own words. Next, give the pairs the two sets of statements, cut up, from resource 3.1 to lay face down on the table. Student A should turn over the first set of statement cards one at a time, each time scanning the text for information. Student B

Choosing appropriate reading strategies

Cycle B

Duration: 1 hour

should use the 'Assess your progress' criteria on page 71 of the Student Book to assess student A, give clear feedback and set a target for the next scan. Hand out the second set of statement cards. Students swap roles and repeat the process.
Plenary (10 minutes)
Finish the lesson by asking the students to articulate the difference between skimming and scanning and to describe an occasion when a reader might need to use each of these skills. Feedback to secure. Which aspects of skimming and scanning do the students feel confident about? What aspects of these processes do they still feel unsure of?

Lesson Plan
1 of 3

Making judgements about texts

Competent reader

Cycle C

Duration: 1 hour

Resources needed	Lesson aims	Assessment Focuses
• Student Book pages 72–73: 'Making a deduction' • CD-ROM Cycle C (Competent reader) resource sheets 1.1 and 1.2: cut-up cards	• to be able to infer and deduce meanings from texts • to be able to comment on evidence found in a text **Target areas** • Target area 1: Reading between the lines	AF2, AF3, AF5

Starter (15 minutes)

Tell the students to look at pages 72–73 of the Student Book. Give them one minute to remember the iceberg of meaning. Ask: 'What is it? How does it work?' Students pair and share what they remember. As a class, clarify literal and non-literal meanings of texts. In this lesson, students will develop their deduction skills. Explain that the words above the iceberg are taken from a text. Take one of the key words and, speaking aloud using the stems provided, model the process of defining the literal meaning of the word and then investigating the non-literal meanings. In pairs, students continue the process with the other key words, being sure to use the stems. After five minutes, explain that you are going to have a go at making a deduction: can the students remember the sum format they used when they first learnt how to do this? Model the process of making links between two of the words and making a deduction: what is this text about? Give the students a chance to make similar links and then ask individuals to explain their own deductions. Record them clearly on the board for later use.

Introduction (15 minutes)

Explain to the students that they are now going to try to make deductions based on sentences from the mystery text. Model the process of asking questions about the following sentence: 'The wooden planks beneath him bulged and strained.' Use questions beginning with Who/Where/What/When/Why/Which/How, questioning the sentence and recording those questions around the sentence. Give pairs of students copies of the cards on resource sheet 1.1. Students follow the questioning process modelled, recording their questions clearly on the cards.

Take one of the questions that you drew up about the first sentence, and model aloud the process of answering that question. Swap the cards between pairs of students. Give them five minutes to make deductions in answer to the questions. As a class, return to the list of deductions recorded on the board after the first session. Has looking at these sentences given us a clearer idea of what the mystery text is about? As a class, draw the sentences together and make deductions about the whole text, adding to the list on the board.

Development (20 minutes)

As a class, read the entire text on page 73 of the Student Book aloud. To what extent were the students' deductions from the key words and detached sentences correct? Making it clear that you are using your fingers and eyes to scan, model aloud the process of taking one of the students' deductions from the board and scanning for evidence that would support the deduction, before deciding whether the deduction was correct. Working independently, students choose a deduction from the board and practise the process modelled. Organise the students into groups of three for them to share their findings.

Return to the iceberg. What literal information do we have about the man in the boat? Give two minutes for individual students to scan the text for literal information about him and take feedback, recording literal meanings on the board. In their groups of three, students take each of the pieces of literal information and try to take them 'below the waterline'. Give each group the cut-up stems on resource sheet 1.2 to aid this discussion.

Plenary (10 minutes)

Explain to the students that they have improved their ability to deduce/make deductions in this lesson.

Making judgements about texts

Cycle C

Duration: 1 hour

Organise them into pairs. Student A will test their deduction skills, speaking aloud and explaining their thinking; student B will observe how well A does against the success criteria and then give some feedback. The question is: 'Why is this man in the boat?' Run the activity. Student A should then set a personal target for development, aided by student B.

Making judgements about texts

Competent reader

Cycle C

Duration: 1 hour

Resources needed	Lesson aims	Assessment Focuses
• Student Book pages 74–75: 'Making judgements about texts' • CD-ROM Cycle C (Competent reader) resource sheet 2.1: cut-up stems • CD-ROM Cycle C (Competent reader) resource sheet 2.2: table for distribution	• to be able to comment on evidence found in a text • to be able to express personal preferences about texts **Target areas** • Target area 4: Explaining and justifying textual preference	AF2, AF3, AF5

Starter (15 minutes)

Give the class one minute to remember: How are deductions made? Pair and share, checking for agreement. Tell the students to look at page 74 of the Student Book. Clarify 'deduction' as a class, using the success criteria provided. Give students five minutes, working individually, to consider the question in the 'Ask yourself' box with reference to the front cover of *The Life of Pi*, using the success criteria to guide them. Students should make notes in their exercise books, using the question words to help them.

After five minutes, organise the students into groups of three and provide them with the stems on resource sheet 2.1. Tell the students that these stems will help them to explain their ideas: to think before they speak, give information in an ordered way and to speak clearly. Allow five minutes for the students to share their deductions, using the stems. As a class, consider whether you would like to read this book. Model the structure of stating a preference, giving a specific detail to support, then encourage the students to follow: *I would/would not like to read this book because …*

Introduction (15 minutes)

Give the students one minute to think about which part of the success criteria for deducing they find the most difficult at the moment. Take responses, modelling the way that those difficulties could be turned into a target. Students set themselves a target for the next session, beginning 'I will …'. Organise the students into pairs: A and B. A will deduce, speaking their thinking aloud; B will observe and give feedback. Make deductions about the film poster on page 74 of the Student Book, followed by feedback from the observer. Swap roles.

Re-call the attention of the class: now that they have made deductions about the film poster and the book, which story do they prefer and why? Give the students one minute to think about it. They need to have three reasons to back up their preference. Model the use of the stems to explain your choice; make it clear that you are gathering your thoughts before you speak. Ask the class to comment on how you made your verbal explanation clear (*eye contact, pausing between points, etc.*) Give the students an opportunity to present their choice to three other students in the room, as they have been shown.

Development (20 minutes)

In pairs, students read the first text on page 75 of the Student Book and share the questions they have about it. Ask the pairs to choose the question they think is most important; feedback these questions to the board. Individuals should choose three of the questions from the board and, returning to the text, follow the process of making a deduction. Pair and share the students' deductions, making sure that they explain their ideas clearly.

Explain that the second text on the page tells the same story but in a different way. Read the text as a class. Which of these two texts do the students find the most exciting? Give pairs of students copies of the table on resource sheet 2.2. Model the process of scanning the first sentence for exciting words, extracting a word, thinking about why it is exciting and recording the ideas. In pairs, students scan through the sentences of the texts and continue the process.

Plenary (10 minutes)

Making judgements about texts

Cycle C

Duration: 1 hour

Pairs of students reflect on their findings and decide which of the texts they find the most exciting – they do not have to agree. Model the process of explaining which text you find the most exciting, commenting on three of the words in the text and why you find them exciting as support for your view. Hand out prompt cards (resource sheet 2.2) to students who will need support. Give students two minutes to prepare their choice of text, backed up by comments on three specific words. Allow students to share their responses with at least two others in the room.

Making judgements about texts

Competent reader

Cycle C

Duration: 1 hour

Resources needed	Lesson aims	Assessment Focuses
• Student Book pages 76–77: 'Making predictions' • CD-ROM Cycle C (Competent reader) resource sheet 3.1: stems	• to be able to infer and deduce meaning from texts • to be able to use inference to predict and speculate **Target areas** • Target area 2: Using a range of reading strategies	AF2, AF3

Starter (15 minutes)

Using the iceberg of meaning, remind the students that they are learning to read non-literal meaning. One of the ways of getting beneath the waterline of a text is to deduce. In this lesson they will be developing another way of reading beneath the waterline: they will learn to infer, to make inferences about a text. Explain that when we deduce, we make links between bits of information that we can see in the text, drawing conclusions. When we infer, we have to look beneath the literal information, using our feelings, our imagination and our past experiences to understand what is happening.

Give individual students one minute to read the image on page 76 of the Student Book and make a deduction: what is happening in this picture? Students explain their deduction to a partner, including **how** they made it. Using resource sheet 3.1, model aloud the process of making an inference in response to one of the questions above the image. In pairs, students use the stems to make inferences in response to the other question. Feedback the ideas to the class and record them on the board. As a class, group similar responses together but also notice the differences. Explain to the class that when we infer, there is not necessarily a single answer: there are often a number of answers.

Introduction (15 minutes)

Using the first statement underneath the picture on page 76 of the Student Book, model the process of making an inference in response to the question, using the same stems as earlier. In particular, model the process of checking your inference against the sentence by identifying supporting detail. Make it clear that predictions should not be wild guesses: they must be based on detail in the text. Working in pairs, students continue the process to infer meaning from the sentences. Pairs join up into groups of four and share their inferences.

Return the students' attention to the sentences on page 76 of the Student Book. Explain that you are going to show them the final step in the process of inferring: making a prediction; speculating about what might happen next. Using the speculating stems on page 77 of the Student Book, model aloud the process of drawing together some of the inferences made about the image used earlier in the lesson, predicting what will happen next and then checking that prediction by finding supporting detail in the text. Individual students have 2 minutes to use the same process to make a prediction about the narrative being told in the sentences. Pair and share, checking that they can find supporting evidence.

Development (20 minutes)

Organise the students into teams of three, each with a different role; reading, inferring or predicting. The students use the text on page 77 and should rotate their roles after every two sentences. After reading the paragraph, the groups should gather their predictions and make a final prediction about what will happen in the next paragraph, based on their reading of the first. Share these predictions as a class, using the stems on page 77 of the Student Book to back up their predictions. Record the main predictions on the board. As a class, compare the predictions, making links between similar ideas. As a class, read the second paragraph of the text. Give individual students 2 minutes to decide which of the predictions were correct and how they can tell.

Plenary (10 minutes)

Have they enjoyed the text so far? Based on their predictions, would they like to read on? Model the

Making judgements about texts

Cycle C

Duration: 1 hour

process of making a judgement and backing it up with a 'because' and a reference to the text. Allow the students to share their own judgements with at least three other students, listening to the responses of others. Using the images in the right-hand column of page 77 of the Student Book, students should discuss in pairs which image best fits the process of making a prediction. They should discuss each image in turn and then make a decision before feeding back their choice and reasons to the class.

Lesson Plan
1 of 3

Understanding the main purpose of a non-fiction text

Competent reader

Cycle D

Duration: 1 hour

Resources needed	Lesson aims	Assessment Focuses
• CD-ROM Cycle D (Competent reader) resource sheets 1.1 and 1.2: cut-up cards • Student Book pages 78–79: 'What will this text be about?'	• to be able to categorise information into groups • to be able to find information from a text independently • to be able to recognise basic organisation and presentational features of texts **Target areas** • Target area 3: Finding the main ideas in a text and supporting them with evidence	AF2, AF4

Starter (15 minutes)

Ask the students: 'What do we know about paragraphs?' Give them one minute to consider this, then pair/share before feeding back their ideas to the board. If there are misunderstandings, say: 'Well, I'm not sure about that, so I'm going to put a question mark next to it and come back to it during the lesson.' Explain that one of the most important things about paragraphs is that they are a way of grouping similar ideas together so that texts are easier to read.

Hand out cut-up cards on resource sheet 1.1, one per student. Explain to the students that each of their cards shows a different symbol/image. They will be given five minutes to circulate the room and share their image with others in the room: the aim of the game is to group themselves with other students who have a symbol that is linked to their own. After five minutes, stop the class and ask any students still without a group to show their image: as a class, try to place them in a group, asking students to explain the reasons behind their choices as fully as possible. Give the groups one minute to decide exactly how their images are linked: they should come up with an action that explains the link and show this action to the class.

Introduction (15 minutes)

Ask the students to look at page 78–79 of the Student Book: words taken from a text. They need to decide what the text will be about, based on their reading of the words. Allow one minute for individual students to look at all of the words and to decide which reading strategies they will use. Pair and share ideas about **how** to read. Once they have decided which reading strategies they will use and in what order, allow pairs of students two minutes to read the words and make their prediction, speaking aloud their thoughts and connections to one another.

Next, ask individual students to mentally gather what they remember about topic sentences. Pair and share, then take feedback from the class. Return to the list of ideas about paragraphs on the board made earlier in the lesson. Do topic sentences feature in that list? Do they need adding/clarifying? Turn the students' attention to pages 78–79 of the Student Book. Using the description of topic sentences, pairs of students work through the sentences, deciding whether or not they are topic sentences. Begin by modelling the process of interrogating one of the sentences, using the bulleted criteria.

Development (20 minutes)

Organise the students into groups of three and give each group a set of cut-up sentences from resource sheet 1.2. Explain that three of the sentences they have been given are topic sentences and the others come from within the three paragraphs. Allow the students to decide which are topic sentences and then take responsibility for one of the topic sentences each.

The next activity requires the students to work through the remaining sentences as a group, taking just one at a time, and deciding which of the remaining sentences should appear after which topic sentence. If a student thinks a sentence 'belongs' to their topic sentence, they need to explain why by referring to a word in either one of the sentences. You could give them the stem: 'I think that this

Understanding the main purpose of a non-fiction text

Competent reader

Cycle D

Duration: 1 hour

sentence belongs to me because … the word which tells me this is …' If two students claim the same sentence, they must justify their claim; the third team member should help to make the final decision.
Plenary (10 minutes)
Whilst the students are still in their groups of three, use the 'Ask yourself' prompt questions from Student Book page 79 to hold a discussion about the purpose of the text. Deal with one question at a time, allowing one minute's individual thinking time, followed by sharing time, followed by clarification as a class. Encourage students to prompt their team-mates to refer to aspects of the text to support their views by giving the class the question, 'What exactly makes you say that?'

Lesson Plan
2 of 3

Understanding the main purpose of a non-fiction text

Competent reader

Cycle D

Duration: 1 hour

Resources needed	Lesson aims	Assessment Focuses
• CD-ROM Cycle D (Competent reader) resource sheet 2.1: cut-up sentences • Student Book pages 80–81: 'Striking a balance' • CD-ROM Cycle D (Competent reader) resource sheet 2.2: scales worksheet	• to be able to understand the main purpose of a text • to be able to categorise information into groups **Target areas** • Target area 3: Finding the main ideas in a text and supporting them with evidence	AF2, AF4, AF6

Starter (15 minutes)

Give students one minute to remember how to skim, then let them share their thoughts with a partner. Now, as a class, compile advice on the board on how to skim. Explain to the students that they will need to use their skimming techniques in this lesson to identify the main idea in a series of sentences so that these sentences can be grouped together. Using one of the sentences on resource sheet 2.1, model the process of skimming the sentence for meaning, pulling out just the key words so that you can decide what the sentence is about. Make sure that you speak aloud the thought processes involved in this: the need to identify words that give facts, such as nouns.

Now organise the students into pairs and hand out the remaining sentence strips; pairs should deal with the sentences one at a time, taking turns to skim for the key words and making a decision about the content of the sentence. The students should speak their thoughts aloud, as they were shown.

Introduction (15 minutes)

Tell the students that the sentences they have been given come from three paragraphs of a text. Remind them that each paragraph will be organised around one 'big' point or topic. Give them four minutes to organise the sentences into three groups. The rule of this activity is that if a student touches a sentence strip, they must explain their thinking using the stems 'I think … because …' and 'I am wondering if … because …' Once the sentences have been grouped into three sections, join pairs of students into groups of four so that they can compare their decisions on where they have placed the sentences. Feedback any disagreements to the board and ask the class to help sort them out: justifications must be backed up with a reference to the information in the sentences.

Explain that because these sentences and paragraphs are from a non-fiction text, they can be given sub-headings that explain their content. Model the process of giving one group of sentences a sub-heading: come up with two possible suggestions and talk aloud the process of choosing the most fitting sub-heading, justifying the decision by referring to details in the sentences. Individual students should come up with sub-headings for the remaining two paragraphs. They should share these ideas with a partner and then, in pairs, choose the most fitting sub-heading, making sure that they can justify their choice by referring to detail in the sentences.

Development (20 minutes)

Turn to page 81 of the Student Book. Explain to students that the sentences they have been working with were taken from this text: an advert for a scuba-diving course. Explain that adverts are often made up of two types of writing: information about the product being sold and persuasion encouraging the reader to buy it. Look at page 80 of the Student Book and explain the thinking behind the 'scales' illustration. Model the process of taking a word/phrase and categorising it as either information or persuasion. Take a word or phrase from around the scales and ask: 'Which side of the scales should this word/phrase lie, and why?' Model aloud the thought processes involved.

Organise the students into pairs: A and B. A will decide which side of the scales a word/phrase lies on; B will question them, using the prompt questions on page 80 of the Student Book and making sure that they receive a satisfactory explanation. Take brief feedback: were any of the phrases difficult to place and, if so, why? Hand out a copy of the 'scales' worksheet, one per pair (resource sheet 2.2). Turn the students' attention to the actual text: taking the first paragraph, a sentence at a time, model the process of extracting the key words and phrases and placing them on either side of the scales,

Understanding the main purpose of a non-fiction text

Cycle D

Duration: 1 hour

speaking aloud the thought processes. In pairs, continuing to swap roles after each sentence, students should continue to read and categorise the rest of the text, recording the key words and phrases on their copy of the worksheet.

Plenary (10 minutes)

Lead a discussion around the following big questions: 'What is the main purpose of this text? Is the main purpose of this text to give information? Or is it to persuade us to buy this scuba-diving course?' Give individual students two minutes to review their copy of the set of scales and to re-read the text, deciding which response they will make. Give them the stems below to help scaffold their verbal response, and then allow them the opportunity to practise their explanation with at least three other students in the room, listening to their peers' responses: *For me, the main purpose of this text is … I think this because … When I read this text I …* End the lesson by asking students to clarify what we mean by the 'main purpose' of a text.

Lesson Plan 3 of 3	Infer and deduce meaning from non-fiction texts, making judgements	Competent reader

Cycle D

Duration: 1 hour

Resources needed	Lesson aims	Assessment Focuses
• Student Book pages 82–85: 'Anyone for scuba?' • CD-ROM Cycle D (Competent reader) resource sheets 3.1 and 3.2: sentence analysis	• to be able to understand the main purpose of a text • to be able to recognise basic organisation and presentational features of texts **Target areas** • Target area 4: Explaining and justifying textual preference	AF4, AF5, AF6

Starter (15 minutes)

Using pages 82–83 of the Student Book, turn the students' attention to the images from scuba-diving adverts. Make sure that students know what an advert is and where they might see adverts in the world around them. Hold a brief discussion about where they might find images like these, advertising scuba-diving holidays. Using the prompt questions on page 82 of the Student Book, model a response to one of the images, making sure that details are referred to and explained. In pairs, students respond to the remaining images.

Round off this activity by encouraging students to make and justify a decision about which image is most successful in advertising scuba diving to them. Model the process first by choosing an image and giving two reasons to support your decision, referring to and explaining details from the image.

Introduction (15 minutes)

Hand out the cut-up strips numbered 1–5 on resource sheet 3.2 (print each set on different coloured card if possible). Organise the students into pairs. Hand out the strips and use the questions on resource sheet 3.1 on the projector to model the process of analysing the effects of the first two sentences and making a personal choice about the most persuasive sentence. Pairs of students analyse the pairs of sentences in the same way. Once the students have analysed all of the sentences and made their choices, they should place all of their choices together in order and read the 'advert' through aloud to one another. Are they happy with their choices and the overall advert? Do they want to make some changes?

Development (20 minutes)

Organise the students into pairs and allow them four minutes to read through the scuba advert on page 84 of the Student Book: one student reads a sentence aloud, then the other student comments on the word in that sentence that most makes them want to scuba dive. Introduce the idea that different types of texts have different ingredients and shapes. Point out the five text features in the boxes around the outside of the advert – most written adverts have these features. Give individual students two minutes to decide which feature relates to which part of the advert. In pairs, the students compare their responses. Take feedback – is there any disagreement or confusion? Turn the students' attention to the jumbled advert on page 85 of the Student Book. In pairs, using their new knowledge of how an advert is organised, can they put this text back together? Join pairs into groups of four to explain the order in which they have re-built the advert. Model the process of explanation by using the following stems: *We decided to begin with … because … Next we have put … because …*

Plenary (10 minutes)

Remind the class that both the texts they have been reading are adverts. They have been written in order to sell something, to persuade the reader to buy something. Ask: 'Which of these adverts do you think is the most successful and why?' Give individual students two minutes to read back through both adverts and to make an initial decision. They should have three reasons to support their choice. In pairs, using the stems on page 85 of the Student Book, students share their preferences and the reasons behind them. Next, ask students if, in the light of what their partner said, they have changed their minds. If so, give them a further 30 seconds to reorganise their thoughts before pairing up with a

Infer and deduce meaning from non-fiction texts, making judgements

Competent reader

Cycle D

Duration: 1 hour

different student to explain their preference and reasons again.

Lesson Plan
1 of 3

Reading between the lines: Consolidation and assessment

Competent reader

Assessment

Duration: 1 hour

Resources needed	Lesson aims	Assessment Focuses
• Teacher's Guide page 112: visual prompt cards • Student Book page 86–87: 'Active reader!' • CD-ROM Cycle A (Competent reader) resource sheets 2.2: iceberg image	• to independently use a range of imaginative reading strategies • to be able to use clues from the text to work out what a writer means, even when it is not stated directly **Target areas** • Target area 1: Reading between the lines • Target area 2: Using a range of reading strategies	AF3

Starter (15 minutes)

Using the visual prompt cards on page 112 of the Teacher's Guide, ask pairs of students to remind themselves of the reading strategies they can now use when reading a fiction text. Feedback to the class to clarify. Draw attention to the stems at the bottom of page 86. Explain that these are the kinds of things that a reader might say or write in response to a text. Give the pairs one minute to practise saying the stems aloud; take some feedback on which of the stems the students feel comfortable with and which they remember having used when responding to a text in an earlier lesson.

Next, model the thought processes involved in taking one of the stems and deciding which reading strategy it is linked with. Allow the pairs of students three minutes to continue this process, categorising the stems beneath the reading strategies. Pairs join up into groups of four to compare the way they have sorted the stems: are there any disagreements? Deal with any of the stems the class is confused with, making sure that you clarify the reading strategies as you explain. Finally, ask students to decide which of the reading strategies they feel most comfortable using and which they feel that they need to practise.

Introduction (15 minutes)

Turn to page 86–87 of the Student Book. Explain to the students that you want them to be more independent in this lesson: they are going to test out the reading strategies they have been learning to use. Which reading strategy will help them to discover most about the meaning of this text? Hand out a copy of the iceberg of meaning (resource sheet 2.2) one per pair. Give students one minute to remind themselves of the significance of the iceberg: what does it have to do with reading? Clarify as a class. Explain to the students that they are going to record the findings of their reading of the text on the iceberg. Read the text through as a class.

Taking 'visualising' as the first reading strategy, model the process of visualising from the words in the first sentence in the text and thinking through the ideas this raises. Finish the process by asking students to record any interesting ideas this has raised on their iceberg, below the waterline, writing a 'V' for visualising in brackets after the note. In pairs, the students should continue to use the visualising strategy to read the remaining sentences of the text, recording any important ideas they find with a 'V' in brackets. If they want to, they can use the stems from the beginning of the lesson to help them frame their ideas.

At the end of the activity, recall the class and ask them how successful they found visualising to be as a first reading strategy. What kinds of meanings did it allow them to find?

Development (20 minutes)

Still in pairs, students work through the remaining reading strategies, one at a time, each time recording important ideas below the waterline of the iceberg with a code in brackets so that they can keep track of which strategy allowed them to uncover which meaning. At the end of the activity, use the 'Ask yourself' questions on Student Book page 87 to evaluate the findings and the success of the strategies, giving one minute's thinking time, one minute's pair and share time, followed by whole-class discussion for each question. End this session by asking the students to set themselves two

Reading between the lines: Consolidation and assessment

Assessment

Duration: 1 hour

personal targets for using reading strategies, beginning with, 'I will …'. Record these targets for use in the next lesson.

Plenary (10 minutes)

Return to the idea of the iceberg: literal, obvious meanings should be above the waterline. Deeper, more hidden, non-literal meanings should go below the waterline. Model the process of sharing a non-literal meaning from the text, picking out the clue that led to the meaning and explaining which reading strategy helped to get there. Explain to the pairs of students that you are going to give them two minutes to prepare their own explanation of a deep meaning of the text. They should use the following stems to help guide them: *One of the deeper meanings in this text is … I was led to this meaning by a clue in the text … To reach this meaning, I used …* Join up pairs of students into groups of four and allow them to share their readings: does the opposite pair agree that this is a non-literal meaning? Do they have any questions about the meaning?

Competent reader

Starter activity: visual prompt cards

Visualising • When you read this text, what do you 'see' or imagine? • Which words and phrases create the strongest images for you?	**Empathising** • When you read this text, which bits do you most like? Which ideas do you most easily understand? • Is there anything in the text that you dislike or ideas that you don't understand? • Can you understand what the characters in the text are doing and thinking? Would you want to be in their shoes?
Predicting and speculating • What do you already know about this topic that might help you understand the text? • Have you come across a story like this before? • What do you think might happen in this story and what are the clues that tell you?	**Asking questions** • When you read this text, what more do you want to find out? • Is there anything that puzzles or interests you? • What 5W questions would it be useful to ask to find out more about events and characters? (Who, What, Where, When, Why)

Lesson Plan 2 of 3

Reading between the lines: Consolidation and assessment

Competent reader

Assessment

Duration: 1 hour

Resources needed	Lesson aims	Assessment Focuses
• Student Book pages 88–89: 'Betrayal' • Teacher's Guide page 115: cut-up sentences	• to be able to independently use a range of reading strategies • to be able to find the main ideas in a text and support them with evidence **Target areas** • Target area 1: Reading between the lines • Target area 2: Using a range of reading strategies	AF2, AF3

Starter (15 minutes)

Return to personal targets from the previous lesson, sharing and understanding them. Students will now have an opportunity to meet these targets. They will independently apply reading strategies to new sections of the text and record their findings on the iceberg of meaning. Use the 'Remind yourself" questions on page 88 to recap on the story so far. Students should make a list of questions about things they don't understand and want to find out about. Organise students into pairs to discuss and share their findings; ask: 'Can your partner help you to answer some of the questions?'

Introduction (15 minutes)

Ask: 'How is the narrator/teller of this story feeling and why?' Point out that this type of question will require the students to read below the waterline and look for non-literal meaning. Organise the students into pairs and hand out one of the cut-up sentences from page 115 of the Teacher's Guide. Model the process of taking a sentence and deducing the narrator's feelings, making sure that you check your deduction by placing the sentence back into the context of the whole text to make sure that your idea makes sense. Give pairs of students one minute to discuss the feelings of the narrator in their sentence: they need to decide on the main emotion the narrator is feeling and be able to explain which particular word in the sentence led them to their decision. They should also check whether their deduction makes sense by considering it in the light of the rest of the text.

Use a 'statues' game to exemplify the emotions conveyed by the text: one of the students is a lump of clay, the other is a sculptor. The sculptor needs to create a statue with their chosen emotion as the title. Ask the students to show their statues; 'clap' the statues alive for a couple of seconds, so that the statue can speak aloud the word of the quotation most powerful in communicating the narrator's emotion. Repeat this process a number of times, swapping the sentences being analysed each time and ensuring that the clay/sculptor roles are also swapped.

Using the 'Assess your progress' box on page 89 of the Student Book, model the process of writing a short paragraph in response to one of the quotations that have been explored. You could use the following stems: *the man is feeling … he feels like this because … we can tell this when …* Ask students to use the success criteria to assess your paragraph and to point out the successful features of the response.

Development (20 minutes)

Using the 'Assess your progress' prompts to guide them, students have a go at responding to the questions: 'How is the narrator feeling? Why?' Give students two minutes to work individually, choosing a sentence from the resource sheet on page 115 of the Teacher's Guide to respond to, gathering their thoughts and finding their key word for evidence. Organise the students into groups of three; they should take turns to state their responses while the other two students use the success criteria to assess the success of the response and set a target for the next response. Recall the class – ask groups to share the successes and development targets of some of their group members. Next allow individual students 10 minutes to take a further two or three sentences from the text to respond to, this time recording their ideas in writing. Allow the students to have a go at first without stems and then offer support to those who need it.

Reading between the lines: Consolidation and assessment

Assessment

Duration: 1 hour

Plenary (10 minutes)
Explain to the students that you are going to mark their responses to this text, so that you can see how much progress they have made in their use of inference and deduction. Run some peer assessment of the written responses by asking students to swap their work. They should use the success criteria to identify successes in the responses and feed these successes back to their partner verbally. One target area should be identified. Allow a further three minutes to make any final improvements. Finally, ask students what aspect(s) of their reading they feel have got better over the past few weeks: give one minute's thinking time before sharing reflections with one another. What do they still find hard? Take feedback.

Competent reader

What is the narrator feeling?

My mind was spinning.
For this I would never be forgiven.
If the information on the map I held in my hand was correct, I would never need anybody ever again.
It was he who had found me the tiny room in the university grounds where I slept each night.
I was standing on the knife-edge of the biggest decision I had ever made.
What if I had made an error in my calculations?
What if the map itself was incorrect?
These questions multiplied with great speed and chewed my calm like jagged teeth.

Reading between the lines: Consolidation and assessment

Competent reader

Assessment

Duration: 1 hour

Resources needed	Lesson aims	Assessment Focuses
• Student Book pages 90–91: 'A struggle of the mind' • Cut-up pieces of blank paper: five per student • Teacher's Guide page 118: symbols	• to be able to read between the lines • to be able to make and explain a personal response to a text **Target areas** • Target area 1: Reading between the lines • Target area 4: Explaining and justifying textual preference	AF3

Starter (15 minutes)

Recap: give each student five small pieces of blank paper and 90 seconds' thinking time to cast their mind back over the story so far and jot down three main points in answer to the question: 'What has happened in the story so far?' Organise students into groups of four. They should use their pieces of paper like playing cards, keeping them hidden from the rest of their group. Taking turns, students choose one of their pieces of paper and say, 'In this story ...'. The rest of the group look at their own responses and decide whether they also made this response (even though the wording might be different). All similar responses should be placed in a pile, face up, on the table. The students should continue taking turns. Praise any student who remembers something about the plot of the story that no-one else did.

Next, students should try to order the events of the story, using their cards. Give them five minutes, working in their groups of four, to create between three and five freeze-frames of the events of the story so far. They should begin by deciding how many freeze-frames they will need to tell the story, before discussing and creating the detail. The only rule is that every member of the team needs to be physically involved in each freeze-frame. Allow each group two run-throughs of their sequence of freeze-frames, counting them down to freeze and telling them when to create the next freeze-frame each time. See some of the sequences of freeze-frames and ask members of the class to deduce which parts of the story they are viewing at different points and how they can tell.

Introduction (15 minutes)

Explain to the students that this text deals with a problem. Give individual students one minute to consider the question: 'What is this central problem?' Students share ideas in their group of four and then feedback their group's responses to the class. Use the tug-of-war-rope on page 90–91 of the Student Book to clarify the central problem: the narrator is trying to decide whether or not to betray the old man. Organise the students into pairs and give a symbols resource sheet (page 118 of the Teacher's Guide) to each pair. Model aloud the thought process involved in taking one of the sentences on that page and deciding which side of the tug of war it should go on. Pairs of students continue this process, making sure that they explain their ideas clearly and challenge one another if they do not agree. Check understanding by reading the sentences aloud and, giving the students 10 seconds' conferring/thinking time, ask them to hold up the correct card: betray the old man or be true to him.

Working more independently, pairs of students should turn to the paragraph they read in the previous lesson, beginning, 'I was standing on the knife-edge of the biggest decision I have ever made,' and continue the process by finding a further point for each side of the dilemma. They should write their finding on the back of the correct symbol card and practise speaking the phrase/sentence aloud. Create a tug-of-war tunnel, with students holding the 'betrayal' symbol on one side of the tunnel and students holding the 'stay true' symbol on the other, allowing students to pass through the tunnel having the quotations from the text spoken to them as they move through the tunnel. Hold a discussion: 'What does it feel like to walk down that tunnel? How must the narrator feel?'

Development (20 minutes)

Lesson Plan
3 of 3

Reading between the lines: Consolidation and assessment

Competent reader

Assessment

Duration: 1 hour

Remind the students that one of the skills they have learned recently is to make a personal response to a text, explaining a preference about it. Using the prompts on page 91 of the Student Book, remind them of the success criteria for making a personal response. Their question is: 'Should the narrator enter the cave without the old man?' Give individual students two minutes to review the information in the text and come to an initial decision. Using the stems, *In my opinion .... I think this because ...* model the process of expressing your view in answer to the question. Organise the students into groups of four and play a version of the 'shopping bag' game, beginning with one student expressing their view, and next student adding their own view to create a chain of personal responses: *Sally thinks ... because ....; Sam thinks ... because ... I agree with ____ because ...*

Ask the students to use the success criteria on page 91 of the Student Book to assess how successful the class has been so far in expressing a personal response. Ask: 'What else do we need to do?' Give students four minutes to record their personal response to the question in writing, using the success criteria to guide them. Explain to the students that you are going to mark their responses, so that you can see how well they are able to express a personal response to a text. Run some peer-assessment of the written responses by asking students to swap their work. They should use the success criteria to identify successes in the responses and feed these successes back to their partner verbally. One target area should be identified. Allow the students a further three minutes to make any final improvements.

Plenary (10 minutes)

Return to page 91 of the Student Book and read the remaining paragraph of the story as a class. Remind the students of the success criteria for making a prediction. Allow students two minutes to think individually, jotting down any ideas that they have. In pairs, students verbalise their predictions, give feedback using peer-assessment, and set targets. Meanwhile the teacher can use this time to assess the prediction skills of a targeted group of students.

Reading between the lines:
Consolidation and assessment

Competent reader

Assessment

Duration: 1 hour

Symbols for photocopying

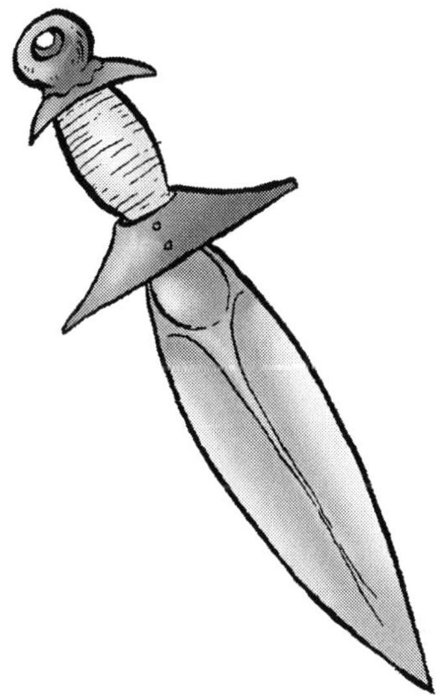

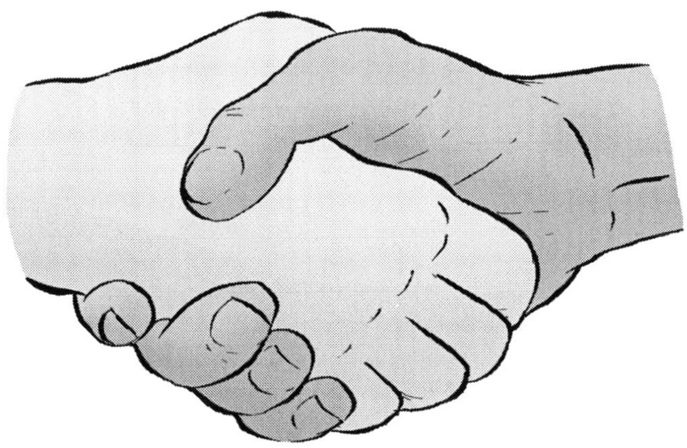

To infer and deduce meanings supported by textual reference

Secure competent reader

Cycle A

Duration: 1 hour

Resources needed	Lesson aims	Assessment Focuses
• Student Book pages 92–93: 'Making notes' • CD-ROM Cycle A (Secure competent reader) resource sheets 1.1: cut-up cards • CD-ROM Cycle A (Secure competent reader) resource sheet 1.2: question sheet • CD-ROM Cycle A (Secure competent reader) resource sheet 1.3: note-maker table	• to be able to annotate a text, making notes for later use • to be able to use inference to predict and speculate about a character's actions **Target areas** • Target area 1: Inference and deduction	AF3

Starter (15 minutes)

Organise the students into pairs and get them out of their seats. As a warm-up, use a 'statues' game, where one student is a 'lump of clay' and the other is the sculptor, with 1 minute each time to mould the clay to suit a title for the statue. The titles should be: Strength, Bravery, Kindness, Truth. Next, give each pair one of the cut-up cards from resource sheet 1.1. Pairs should come up with a freeze-frame that shows the story told on their card; both students should be involved in the frozen picture. They should think about using every bit of their body – right down to the tips of their fingers – to communicate the story. Show the first freeze-frame to the class and model inferring what is happening, then speculate about what the character will do next based on those inferences. You could use the following stems to frame this process: *I notice (refer to a detail of the freeze-frame) ... this makes me think (inference about what is happening) ... So, I wonder if ... (speculation)* Using the other freeze-frames, ask the students to continue this process as a class, inviting contributions from individuals, rather than allowing students to call out.

Introduction (15 minutes)

Turn to pages 92–93 of the Student Book and explain the new skill that the students will be learning: making notes **as they read** for future use. Using the image from the film *Braveheart*, ask the students: 'Who is the hero in this image, and how can you tell?' Ask them to remind you how to make a deduction and clarify this on the board for those who are unsure. The students will need to use their deduction skills to answer this question. Give one minute's reading/thinking time before pairing and sharing ideas, being sure to be really clear about how the deduction has been made. Model the process of taking one of the annotations and deciding which detail in the picture it stems from. In pairs, students continue this activity, making sure that they speak their thoughts aloud.

Recall the students' attention. Ask: 'Which of these annotations were difficult to place and why?' Return to the question; model the process of identifying one annotation that is useful in helping to answer the question and one annotation that is not useful, explaining aloud your thought processes fully. Give individual students one minute to choose one annotation that they think is useful in answering the question and one annotation that is not useful. Take suggestions from the class, with clear explanations. To draw out the learning here, turn to the success criteria for making notes in the Student Book. Read them as a class – which do they think will be the most difficult? Which is the most important? Can they add to these success criteria?

Development (20 minutes)

Using the image from resource sheet 1.2 individual students make notes on the image in answer to the questions. Point out that there are three questions this time – the students decide how to organise their notes: either using a different colour for each question or recording their responses in different places on the page. They should also use the success criteria to make sure that their notes are good quality, because they will need to use them in the next part of the lesson. After seven minutes, organise the students into groups of three. Dealing with one question at a time, the students use their notes to answer the questions.

To infer and deduce meanings supported by textual reference

Secure competent reader

Cycle A

Duration: 1 hour

Plenary (10 minutes)
Using resource sheet 1.3, students swap sheets and peer-assess their partner's notes, using the success criteria in the 'Assess your progress' box in the Student Book before giving feedback on what has been done well. Students should set a personal target for note-making in future lessons.

To infer and deduce meanings supported by textual reference

Secure competent reader

Cycle A

Duration: 1 hour

Resources needed	Lesson aims	Framework Objectives
• Student Book pages 94–95: 'The writer's choices' • CD-ROM Cycle A (Secure competent reader) resource sheet 2.1: prompts to support students • CD-ROM Cycle A (Secure competent reader) resource sheet 2.2: copy of first verse of poem, one per student	• to be able to annotate a text, making notes for later use • to be able to comment on a writer's use of language **Target areas** • Target area 2: Using textual evidence to support inference	Y7: R4, R12 **Assessment Focuses** AF3, AF5

Starter (15 minutes)

Using the bullets on the left of page 94 of the Student Book, explain the learning objective and what the students will get better at over the course of the lesson. Organise the students into groups of three. Model the process of reading one of the 'speculate' key phrases at the top of the page, annotating your ideas about what the phrase might mean. Be clear that you are reading beneath the waterline by using phrases like 'This suggests to me …', 'This could mean …' and 'If I look beneath the surface of this word, I see …'. Give each group another one of the key phrases. Allow two minutes for them to read beneath the surface of this phrase, annotating their ideas. Next, give the students three minutes to create a freeze-frame of their phrase to show to the class; two of the students should build the freeze-frame whilst the third student prepares to explain the thinking behind it. Equip this third student with the prompt sheet (resource sheet 2.1) to support them in this role. See the freeze-frames and hear the explanations. As a class, try to make connections between the phrases and record these connections and links on the board: can the students predict what this poem will be about? Give individual students one minute to think before asking them to share their speculations with the class using the stems on page 94 of the Student Book.

Introduction (15 minutes)

Read the first verse of the poem with the class: were their speculations about the subject of the poem correct? Allow students to ask any questions that they have about the content of the poem and encourage others in the room to have a go at answering these, before clearing up any confusion yourself. Give each student a copy of resource sheet 2.2. Ask: 'What do these words "do" to the reader?' Model the process of taking the first phrase and use the stems (*makes me feel …, makes me think …, helps me to understand …)* to make a response to the phrase. In pairs, students should continue this process, annotating their ideas on their copy of the first verse of the poem. Join pairs to form groups of four. Students should explain their responses to the different phrases before deciding in their group which of the phrases has the **most** impact on the reader. They need to be able to justify their choice. Take suggestions and explanations from the class.

Development (20 minutes)

Using page 95 of the Student Book, read the next verse of the poem as a class, pointing out that three of the most powerful words chosen by the poet have been omitted. What might these words be? As a class, take the first blank and discuss the words that might fit into the blank. Select three possibilities and model the process of exploring how the different words will impact on the reader. Give individual students one minute to consider which of the possible choices would be most powerful, before allowing them to explain this to the person sitting next to them.

Organise the students into different pairs. Give them three minutes to discuss possible words for the remaining two gaps in the verse before choosing the most powerful words and creating a freeze-frame for each: one student showing the word and the other explaining it and its impact. Again, this student can be supported with the prompt card (resource sheet 2.1). See the freeze-frames and hear the explanations.

Plenary (10 minutes)

Lesson Plan 2 of 3

To infer and deduce meanings supported by textual reference

Secure competent reader

Cycle A

Duration: 1 hour

What is this poem about? Although the students have only read two verses of the poem, what do they think it is saying so far? In pairs, students should read the two verses aloud, using some of their own words to fill the blanks. Give them three minutes to discuss what this poem is saying to them; they need to come up with one firm idea to share with the class. Once they have their idea, they should find three words or phrases in the text that support their idea. Place the following stems on the board and encourage the students to express their findings: *We think that this poem is saying … We think this because … A word that supports this idea is …*

Lesson Plan
3 of 3

To infer and deduce meanings supported by textual reference

Secure competent reader

Cycle A

Duration: 1 hour

Resources needed	Lesson aims	Assessment Focuses
• CD-ROM Cycle A (Secure competent reader) resource sheet 3.1: pair of quotation cards for each student • Student Book page 96–97: 'How can we tell?' • CD-ROM Cycle A (Secure competent reader) resource sheet 3.2: handout • CD-ROM Cycle A (Secure competent reader) resource sheet 3.3: handout • CD-ROM Cycle A (Secure competent reader) resource sheet 3.4: OHT	• to know how to identify features of a writer's use of language • to know how to quote evidence from the text **Target areas** • Target area 2: Using textual evidence to support inference	AF2, AF5

Starter (15 minutes)

Organise the students into pairs and give each student a pair of quotation cards, on resource sheet 3.1. Ask the students if they recognise speech marks: 'Where have you seen these? When do we use them?' Clarify that there are three times when we might use speech marks: when we are writing what someone has said, when we are writing someone's direct thoughts and when we are making a quotation. By the end of this lesson the students will know how to use quotation marks and be able to use a quotation when offering evidence from a text.

Using pages 96–97 of the Student Book, remind the students of the poem that they read in the previous lesson. Read the first two stanzas of the poem aloud as a class. Ask a 'How can we tell …?' question: 'How can we tell that war is noisy?' Explain to the students that you need to find evidence from the first two stanzas to answer this question, so you are going to scan the text looking for words linked with sound or noise. Model the process of scanning to the word *clash* before explaining that you have found some relevant evidence. Model to the class the process of turning the question on its head in order to answer: 'I can tell that war is noisy because the word "clash" has been used.' Explain to the students that 'clash' is evidence taken straight from the text to answer a question, and therefore needs to be placed inside quotation marks. Repeat your explanation aloud, this time with the students raising the quotation marks at the correct time. In pairs, students follow the same process to answer the questions on page 96 of the Student Book, raising their quotations cards when using evidence. Ask for full, rehearsed responses from a few pairs, praising their use of the cards.

Introduction (15 minutes)

Ask the class what they remember about how to annotate a text successfully. Record advice on the board, being explicit about the reasons behind each piece of advice. Organise the students into pairs. Hand out copies of the remaining two verses of the poem (resource sheet 3.2). Allow five minutes for the students to read and annotate these in answer to the question: 'How does this soldier feel about war?'

Once the students have finished annotating the text, explain that as their reading skills improve, they need to be able to find the most powerful words in a text, the words that the writer has chosen specifically. Turn their attention to the questions at the bottom of resource sheet 3.2 and model the thought processes of answering the first two questions. Allow students to leave their seats and 'interview' one another about the most powerful words in the text. They should record the words that their classmates select on the sheet for later use.

Development (20 minutes)

Distribute copies of resource sheet 3.3, one per student. Working individually, students should answer the interview questions for themselves, explaining what the words help them to understand about the

To infer and deduce meanings supported by textual reference

Secure competent reader

Cycle A

Duration: 1 hour

soldier's feelings about war.
Plenary (10 minutes)
As a class, collate all the inferences about the soldier's feelings about war and record them on the board. On a projector, display 'Making a response' on resource sheet 3.4. Model the process of answering the question about the soldier's feelings, using the prompts. Allow the students two minutes to plan their own response – encourage them to 'draft' their responses out loud. They should use their quotation cards to 'frame' their direct quotation. Allow each student to share their responses with three other students in the room, using their cards to show the quotations. End the lesson by asking students what they have learnt in this lesson about finding and using quotations.

Lesson Plan 1 of 3

To infer and deduce meaning in non-fiction texts, supported by evidence

Secure competent reader

Cycle B

Duration: 1 hour

Resources needed	Lesson aims	Assessment Focuses
• Student Book pages 98–101: 'Recording your findings' • CD-ROM Cycle B (Secure competent reader) resource sheets 1.1 and 1.2: copies of organisers	• to be able to confidently retrieve and confirm simple facts • to be able to independently record the findings of research undertaken **Target areas** • Target area : Using textual reference to support inference	AF2

Starter (15 minutes)

Explain to the class that they are going to be reading more than one text today to find out answers to some questions. This is called research. When we research, it is important to record any useful information that we find so that we can use it later on. Use the information on pages 98–99 of the Student Book to introduce the content of the texts. Explain to the students that you are going to give them a choice of how to record the information that they find when researching: organise them into pairs and give each pair a copy of each of the two organisers on resource sheets 1.1 and 1.2. Give pairs two minutes to have a look at the organisers: do they understand how to use them? Which one do they think will help them to record information from the texts most successfully? Pairs should make a choice and be ready to explain the reasons behind their choice to the class.

Model reading the first sentence of the first text aloud to the class: is there any information in the sentence that would help to answer the four key questions? Model the process of extracting the useful information and give students time to record it in their organisers. Pairs of students continue to find information and record it in their organisers. After seven minutes, allow pairs of students to practise using the information to tell another pair the facts about Macnally's tennis victory.

Introduction (15 minutes)

Using page 100 of the Student Book, explain how important it is to be able to select the correct fact from the text when answering a question. Read the facts taken from the two texts. Take one of the key questions on the texts and, using the prompts in the 'Selecting the correct fact' list, model **aloud** the process of finding a fact that fits the question. Working in pairs, students take a question each and scan the list of extracted facts to find a suitable fact. One student should speak aloud their processes, as they have been shown, while the other student follows the prompts, supporting their partner if needed. This should be followed by some brief feedback on how carefully the fact was selected before students swap roles.

Next, pairs of students should follow the same process, answering the questions at the top of page 101 of the Student Book, this time scanning both whole texts for information.

Development (20 minutes)

Explain to the class that a press conference is going to be held so that television and newspaper reporters can interview Ryan about his win. Organise the students into groups of three. Using page 101 of the Student Book, explain the importance of being able to decide whether statements about a text are true or false by finding evidence from the text to support the decision. Point out the questions in the Student Book: reporters will ask Ryan these questions during the press conference. Teams of three students will have some time to prepare his responses, using facts from the text. For the first three minutes, the students should use **only** their organisers from the starter session of the lesson to decide whether the statements are true or false and to prepare Ryan's responses. After this, give them a further five minutes to turn to the full texts to find more information, if they need it.

Now run a class press conference, selecting four confident students to act as a team representing 'Ryan'. The rest of the class can act as reporters, putting their questions to Ryan. The team representing Ryan can have one minute to confer and share ideas in answer to the question before making their response through one member of the team. This role can be rotated around the team. Round off this activity with a discussion about how useful the organisers were in helping the students to respond to the true/false statements. Did the organisers provide them with all the information that

To infer and deduce meaning in non-fiction texts, supported by evidence

Secure competent reader

Cycle B

Duration: 1 hour

they needed? Did they have to go to the text for certain statements? How could the organisers be changed to make them more useful?
Plenary (10 minutes)
Encourage students to reflect on their skills in selecting facts from the text to confirm statements. Allow them a period of time to reflect before pairing them up with a different student to talk through their strengths. They should ask each other questions like, 'What do you find most difficult about finding fitting facts from a text?' Students should set themselves a target for future lessons and articulate this to their partner. Take examples of targets from the class and give advice on how they could be met: 'So, the next time that you … you could …'

Lesson Plan 2 of 3

To infer and deduce meaning in non-fiction texts, supported by evidence

Secure competent reader

Cycle B

Duration: 1 hour

Resources needed	Lesson aims	Assessment Focuses
• Student Book pages 102–103: 'What do we mean by "the structure of a text"?' • CD-ROM Cycle B (Secure competent reader) resource sheet 2.1: cut-up reports	• to be able to identify some organisational and presentational features of texts **Target areas** • Target area 2: Using textual reference to support inference	AF4

Starter (15 minutes)

Explain to the students that by the end of this lesson they will be able to answer an important question that will help them to be more sophisticated readers: 'What do we mean by the "structure" of a text?' Turn to page 102 of the Student Book and use the bulleted list to explain what we mean by the 'structure' of things: the way a sandwich is 'structured' or put together, how the different parts of a hamster's cage relate to one another. Use the first annotated image to model the identification of the structural features of that thing. As a class, take the second image of the sandwich and have a go at describing the structure of the thing shown: model the use of the 'You could say ...' stems as prompts and encourage the students to use them.

Next, individual students should be given two minutes to look at the remaining image and investigate the structure, making a few notes about their thoughts and findings. Pair and share: students explain the structure of the item to a different partner, using the stems to guide them.

Introduction (15 minutes)

Explain to the students that different types of text have different structures: they look different and are put together in different ways. As the students' reading improves, they will begin to learn about the structures of different types of text. By the end of today's lesson, they will understand more about the structure and layout of a newspaper report. Turn to page 103 of the Student Book: it shows the report that they read in the previous lesson about the young tennis player, Ryan Macnally. To one side of the report are annotations describing the structural features of the report. Read these aloud to the students and model the process of taking one of the structural descriptions and matching it with an aspect of the report, explaining clearly why you have matched the two by referring to a word or phrase, e.g. *I think that this is the topic sentence because it tells us who (Macnally), what (Macnally won a match), where (Wimbledon) and when (this afternoon) all in the same sentence in under 21 words*. Give individual students three minutes to read through the report again and continue to match the descriptions with parts of the report; they need to be able to justify their choices by referring to a word or phrase in the text. Pair the students up to share their thoughts and their justifications: do they agree? Deal with any disagreements as a class.

Explain that most newspaper reports have these same features, even though the story may be different. End this session by asking the students to help you to describe the structural features of a newspaper report, using the stems from the starter session. Start them off with: 'To begin with, the report has a headline in bold capital letters. The headline is short.' Encourage the students to join in.

Development (20 minutes)

Explain that most newspaper reports have the same features, even though the story may be different. Explain that you are going to give them another newspaper report, this time reporting on a different story. The structure will be very similar because both texts are newspaper reports. Organise the students into different pairs and give each pair copies of the cut-up report and structural labels (resource sheet 2.1). Give the students five minutes to match the parts of the report to the labels. Suggest that they begin by sorting the features of newspaper reports from extracts of the report itself. Join pairs and allow them to cross-reference their decisions: do they agree on all of the matches? As a class, deal with disagreements and clarify. Next, allow the students five minutes to decide which order the report should go in; they must explain in detail the reasons behind their decisions. Encourage them to organise the cards neatly on the desks, so that others can see clearly the order they have chosen and can read the report through. Give each pair of students a blank sheet of A4 paper for them to place alongside their version of the report so that others may comment and ask questions

To infer and deduce meaning in non-fiction texts, supported by evidence

Secure competent reader

Cycle B

Duration: 1 hour

about their decisions. Allow a few minutes for students to look at three other pairs' versions, noting the differences, making comments and asking questions. They should record all of this on the sheet provided. When the students return to their own version they should read the comments made by their classmates and try to answer any questions that have been posed. Do they want to make any changes to the structure of their own report?

Plenary (10 minutes)

Point out that different texts have different structures: not all texts have headlines, or photographs to illustrate details in the text. But almost all texts have structure, and it is important that the students can identify details about the structure of texts. So, what is structure? Give individual students one minute to come up with a definition and write it down. Students share their definition with a partner. Pairs reword their definition, recording it clearly in writing, ready to share with another pair. Join pairs into groups and share their definitions again; groups of four need to word a definition that they are all happy with: encourage individuals to challenge their team-mates if they don't feel the wording is correct yet. Feedback these definitions as a class. How can we remember what 'structure' means? Take suggestions.

To infer and deduce meaning in non-fiction texts, supported by evidence

Secure competent reader

Cycle B

Duration: 1 hour

Resources needed	Lesson aims	Assessment Focuses
• Student Book pages 104–107: understanding a writer's choice of words and how to record information • CD-ROM Cycle B (Secure competent reader) resource sheet 3.1: copies of text, one per student • plain paper, one piece per student • CD-ROM Cycle B (Secure competent reader) resource sheet 3.2: role-play questions	• to be able to confidently retrieve and confirm simple facts • to be able to independently record the findings of research undertaken • to know how to identify features of a writer's use of language **Target areas** • Target area 2: Using textual reference to support inference	AF2, AF5

Starter (15 minutes)

Explain to the students that in this lesson they will combine a number of their reading skills: they will be identifying some words that have been carefully chosen by a writer and they will be using their research skills to read a range of different texts. Turn to page 104 of the Student Book and, using the information there (the example 'Who FACT' and 'which word?'), model the thought processes involved in choosing different descriptive words to combine with a fact to make that fact seem exciting and dramatic; use 'If ... then ...' as a pattern for your thinking. Ask the class to help you to make the final decision on which word to use.

Now, in pairs, using the other facts and the word bank in the Student Book, students continue to make choices about the words they attach to the what/where/when facts. Round off this activity by compiling suggestions from different pairs: have these facts been made more dramatic and exciting through the use of these words? Point out that writers carefully choose the words that they use: it is not left to chance.

Introduction (15 minutes)

Draw the students' attention to the text on pages 104–105 of the Student Book: the newspaper report from which the facts have been taken. Give each student a copy of resource sheet 3.1. Remind them that a fact is something that can be proved; give individual students three minutes to read through the report and to identify the facts in the newspaper report by underlining them. Allow the students to join into pairs to share their identification of facts: do they agree? Take feedback from the class on any of the details of the report that they disagree on and clarify to clear up misconceptions. Give individual students a further three minutes to identify five words attached to facts that they feel have been chosen by the writer to make the facts seem more exciting and dramatic. Ask for a suggestion of one of these words from the class and, together, elicit responses as to why this word is 'exciting' and 'dramatic'. Pair up the students and allow them to explain their choices – how do these words make the report more exciting and dramatic? They can use the 'Ask yourself' questions on page 105 to help make their responses.

Development (20 minutes)

Recap from previous lessons: the students need to be able to find information from a number of different texts. Turn to pages 106–107 of the Student Book. Explain that Kate has just started Year 10 and has had her first meeting with a careers advisor. Kate is interested in becoming a firefighter. The careers advisor has set her a task before their next meeting: find out more about being a firefighter. Kate has gathered a number of texts to help her research. Ask the class: 'What kinds of information might Kate be looking for as she is researching? What kinds of questions might she have about the job?' Allow two minutes of paired discussion and then feedback questions to the board, making a clear list.

Next, ask the students to consider how Kate might record the answers to these questions in an

Lesson Plan
3 of 3

To infer and deduce meaning in non-fiction texts, supported by evidence

Secure competent reader

Cycle B

Duration: 1 hour

organised way so that they will be useful to her in the future. If Kate was going to use an organiser to record her findings, what might this organiser look like? Again, allow two minutes for students to discuss how an organiser could be designed before taking feedback from the class. Individual students should decide which of the ideas about the organiser they would like to use before actually creating one on plain paper. Stress that appearance is not of huge importance here: they should free-draw so that time isn't wasted. Remind students that they will need to scan for information and what this requires them to do. Individual students should then spend ten minutes scanning the newspaper report and the two additional texts to find information about firefighting, recording it on their organiser.

Plenary (10 minutes)

Pair up the students, giving one member of the pair the interview questions on resource sheet 3.2. Explain that they need to imagine that Kate has returned to the Careers Advisor for her second meeting. The careers advisor is going to ask Kate a few questions about her research into being a firefighter. The student playing Kate should use the notes in their organiser to respond to the questions. Swap roles. End the lesson with some reflection: how successfully did I record the findings of my research? Was the organiser I chose to record my findings helpful? Looking back, should I have designed my organiser in a different way?

Recognising a writer's point of view

Secure competent reader

Cycle C

Duration: 1 hour

Resources needed	Lesson aims	Assessment Focuses
• CD-ROM Cycle C (Secure competent reader) resource sheet 1.1: bingo sheets, one per pupil • Student Book pages 108–109: 'Points of view' • CD-ROM Cycle C (Secure competent reader) resource sheet 1.2: note-making table, one per student	• to be able to understand the writer's viewpoint • to be able to support comments about a text with mainly relevant quotations from or references to the text **Target areas** • Target area 4: Understanding the writer's viewpoint	AF5, AF6

Starter (15 minutes)

Explain to the class that in this lesson they will learn a new and important reading skill: being able to understand the writer's point of view in a text. Give the students one minute's thinking time: what do we mean by someone's 'point of view'? They should come up with three possible ideas. Take three ideas from the class and record them on the board. Model the process of pulling out the similarities between the ideas offered. Organise the students into groups of three so that they can share their ideas; whenever they can see a similarity between their ideas, they should point it out to the other members of their group. After a few minutes, take responses from the groups, gathering the key ideas that they agreed upon. Share a definition of 'point of view' with the class: *someone's personal beliefs and opinions.*

Hand out copies of the bingo sheet (resource sheet 1.1). Explain to the class that they are going to gather the view points of the members of their class on the subject of recycling. Give students one minute to gather their personal views, thoughts and beliefs about recycling. Ask for a response from one of the students and model the process of scanning the bingo card to see if that view is recorded there, including the process of recognising that an individual might not give us the exact words recorded on the card: interpretation may be needed. Allow the students three minutes of discussion, asking and recording one another's opinions of recycling. The winner is the first person to tick off five of the views represented.

Introduction (15 minutes)

Explain to the students that artists often use their paintings to put across their points of view. Give students one minute to gather their prior knowledge of Lord Nelson – have they heard of him? What do they know about him? Pair and share their knowledge. Use page 108 of the Student Book to fill in the background. Take one of the viewpoints expressed; model the process of finding evidence from the first picture to support it and make notes of the findings on the board. Finally, use the stems provided in the Student Book to express your analysis. Give pairs of students two minutes to scan the other picture for evidence that supports that same view, recording notes. Allow more confident/able students to have a go at using the stems provided to express their findings to the class. Organise the pairs into A's, B's and C's: to correspond with the remaining points of view about Nelson. Give them three minutes to scan both images for evidence to support their viewpoint, making notes of their findings. After they have done this, allow one minute for pairs to rehearse their analysis/explanation of their findings, using the stems provided. Finally, organise students into groups of four pairs that have focused on different points of view: they should present their findings as clearly and formally as possible so that they are teaching their audience.

Development (20 minutes)

Explain to the class that it is not only artists who use paintings to put across their point of view; writers also use their writing to put across their view point. Using page 109 of the Student Book, share the success criteria for identifying a writer's viewpoint with the class (in the 'Assess your progress' box), making sure that they understand what is required of them. Read the sentences on page 109 of the Student Book, about Nelson's death from the point of view of one of his men. Take the first of the viewpoints about Nelson and ask: 'Does the writer of these sentences share this view that ______?' Display the note-making table (resource sheet 1.2) on a projector, and model the process of scanning

Recognising a writer's point of view

Secure competent reader

Cycle C

Duration: 1 hour

the sentences for evidence that the writer shares this viewpoint, pulling out key words and phrases, using inference and deduction skills about what they suggest and making notes for later use. Distribute note-making tables to each of the students. Give them five minutes to go through each of the remaining viewpoints on Nelson, deciding whether the writer of the sentences shares that viewpoint. Using the notes made on the projector and reminding the students of the success criteria, model the process of turning the notes into a written paragraph about the viewpoint, beginning: 'This writer believes …' Make sure that the paragraph is clearly written on the board. Allow pairs of students one minute to assess the paragraph against the success criteria: what have you done well? Next, allow four minutes for individual students to choose the viewpoint they think is strongest in the written sentences and craft their own paragraph.
Plenary (10 minutes)
Students should swap books and peer-assess the mini-paragraphs written, using the success criteria to identify strengths. Allow two minutes spoken feedback to a partner, insisting that they talk about what has been done well by using the success criteria. Return to the term *point of view*. Using the images and questions at the bottom of page 109 of the Student Book, clarify the phrase 'point of view'. Ask the students to choose the image they feel best represents it and ask them to explain to a partner why they have chosen this image.

Lesson Plan
2 of 3

Recognising a writer's point of view

Secure competent reader

Cycle C

Duration: 1 hour

Resources needed	Lesson aims	Assessment Focuses
• CD-ROM Cycle C (Secure competent reader) resource sheet 2.1: starter activity on paraphrasing • CD-ROM Cycle C (Secure competent reader) resource sheet 2.2: OHT • CD-ROM Cycle C (Secure competent reader) resource sheet 2.3: cut-up questions • Student Book page 110–111: 'Support your understanding of a writer's point of view'	• to be able to understand a writer's viewpoint • to understand how to paraphrase or retell, to support comment **Target areas** • Target area 4: Understanding the writer's viewpoint	AF2, AF5, AF6

Starter (15 minutes)

Explain to the students that when we make comments about a text we must support them/back them up. We can do this in different ways: sometimes we might make a direct quotation by taking a key word from the text. Sometimes, when there is a chunk of the text that we want to use as evidence, we do something called paraphrasing. This means that we summarise or retell a relevant part of the text to support our point or idea. Display resource sheet 2.1 on a projector. Model the process of matching the first detail to a suitable paraphrase and explain carefully the relationship between the two. In pairs, students continue to match items from the two columns, making sure that they are clear which of the two is the paraphrase. Next, read aloud the story on resource sheet 2.2. Give each student a question on the story from resource sheet 2.3. Leaving their seats, students ask one another their questions and listen to each others' answers. After two questions and answers, read the story aloud for the final time, before allowing students to ask and answer two final questions. Students should use the prompts at the bottom of the question cards to help them use paraphrase to back up their understanding of the text.

Introduction (15 minutes)

Remember: what do we mean when we talk about a writer's viewpoint? Allow students 30 seconds to think about this before sharing their thoughts with a partner, followed by clarification as a class. Re-use the images on page 108–109 of the Student Book if the students need more reminding. Remind them that in the last lesson they were reading some points of view about Lord Nelson. As a class, read the text on page 110 of the Student Book. Use the example in the Student Book to show how a question can be answered and supported using a paraphrase of the text, rather than by quoting words or phrases directly. Take the second question on the text and model the process of scanning the text for possible answers before expressing the idea and supporting it with a paraphrase beginning, 'I can tell this when …' Give pairs of students five minutes to repeat the process with the next three questions.

Development (20 minutes)

Individually, students read the second text on page 111 of the Student Book. Using the steps in the 'Ask yourself' list, they should work through the first two questions again independently. Pair the students up and allow them to share their responses to the first two questions. Give the students one minute to explain to their partner which of the steps they are finding the most challenging and encourage them to give each other advice. Gather the attention of the class, ask them to share the parts of the process that they are finding difficult and provide them with any guidance they need to continue. Individually, students continue to answer the questions, this time in writing. Again, pair the students to share answers. This time, partners should also check whether the evidence found is paraphrase, rather than direct quotation.

Plenary (10 minutes)

Lesson Plan
2 of 3

Recognising a writer's point of view

Secure competent reader

Cycle C

Duration: 1 hour

Return to the concept of viewpoint. Point out to the class that the writers of these two texts have very different views of Nelson. The writer of the first text believes that Nelson was a hero: he was a good man, he was brave and he was loved by his men. Ask the class: 'How are the views of the second writer different from the views of the first?' Give individual students one minute to gather their thoughts, come up with and consider an answer. Reminding them of the stems on page 109 of the Student Book, allow them to share their initial thoughts with a partner. Can they find evidence in the text to support their understanding of the viewpoint on Nelson expressed in the second text? Using the success criteria from last lesson (page 109 of the Student Book) ask the students to orally draft a paragraph together about the writer's viewpoint on Nelson, paraphrasing a part of the text or using a quotation to support their understanding.

Lesson Plan 3 of 3

Recognising a writer's point of view

Secure competent reader

Cycle C

Duration: 1 hour

Resources needed	Lesson aims	Assessment Focuses
• Student Book pages 112–113: 'Communicating a viewpoint' • CD-ROM Cycle C (Secure competent reader) resource sheets 3.1 and 3.2: annotation • six blank pieces of paper, playing card size, per pair of students	• to understand the writer's viewpoint • to be able to make some comments about the effects and purpose of a writer's choice of language **Target areas** • Target area 3: Identifying and commenting on a writer's choice of language • Target area 4: Understanding the writer's viewpoint	AF5, AF6

Starter (15 minutes)

Turn to page 112 of the Student Book: a series of images and words. In pairs, students should answer the first question together, discussing the reasons behind their decisions. After building their confidence in this way, give individual students two minutes to think about the second question. Students pair and share their responses with a different partner. Point out that most writers choose words and images to put across their viewpoint, their thoughts, opinions and beliefs. As good readers, we need to consider what the writer's viewpoint is and how it has been put across to us.

Introduction (15 minutes)

Explain to the students that they are going to read a third and final text about the death of Nelson in order to deepen their understanding of how to identify a writer's viewpoint. Point out the two statements about the viewpoint of the writer of this text on page 113 of the Student Book: the students' job will be to work out whether they think that these statements are true or false. Display resource sheet 3.1 on a projector and read the first paragraph of the text aloud. Model aloud the thought processes involved in taking a sentence at a time and looking for evidence to support the two statements, identifying key words and phrases and recording them in the table on the projector. At the end of the paragraph, summarise your findings, beginning: 'So, what can we say about the writer's viewpoint on Nelson's death in this text?' Hand out copies of the table on resource sheet 3.2, one per student. Pairs of students should continue to analyse the second paragraph of the text together, taking turns to identify key words and phrases that communicate a viewpoint. Finally, students should work independently on the final paragraph. Allow them one minute to consider: 'What is this writer's viewpoint on the death of Nelson?' Take feedback from the class, encouraging students to offer evidence to support their ideas.

Development (20 minutes)

Turn to page 113 of the Student Book: the quotations from the text. Explain that the phrases extracted from the text have been chosen because the language used by the writer in these sentences helps to show how the sailors feel about their captain. Model the thought processes involved in taking the first extract and identifying the words in it which show the men's feelings for Nelson, eventually identifying the most powerful word. Organise the students into pairs and give each pair six blank pieces of paper, roughly playing-card sized. The pairs should follow the same thought processes to identify the key word from each of the remaining sentences, recording each of their chosen words on a piece of paper. Model the process of placing some of the words on the continuum on page 113 of the Student Book – the thoughts involved in deciding whether one word shows more feeling than the next. Allow a few minutes for pairs to continue this sorting process, using their chosen key words.

Plenary (10 minutes)

Share with the students the success criteria in the 'Assess your progress' box on page 113 of the Student Book for commenting on a writer's use of language. Set up peer-assessment by joining pairs into groups of four: pairs take it in turns to explain two of their choices of word to their audience, while the listeners assess their explanation against the success criteria and give positive feedback. Pairs

Recognising a writer's point of view

Secure competent reader

Cycle C

Duration: 1 hour

swap roles. Before the end of the lesson, all students should set a personal target for commenting on a writer's use of language and share this with a partner.

Lesson Plan 1 of 3

To know how to identify and comment on writers' purposes and use of language

Secure competent reader

Cycle D

Duration: 1 hour

Resources needed	Lesson aims	Assessment Focuses
• Student Book pages 114–117: 'Can you choose a relevant quotation?' • CD-ROM Cycle D (Secure competent reader) resource sheet 1.1: questions and prompts, one per pupil	• to be able to support comments about a text with mainly relevant quotations from or references to the text • to understand how to paraphrase or retell, to support comment **Target areas** • Target area : Using textual reference to support inference	AF2

Starter (15 minutes)

Ask the students what they remember about the word 'relevant'. What does it mean? Give them one minute to think before feeding back to the class. Explain to the students that, as they develop as readers, they need to be able to select relevant quotations to back up their points: their evidence must **fit** the point that they are trying to make.

Turn to page 114 of the Student Book. Use the first exercise at the top of the page to model the selection of the relevant quotations to support the point: think aloud the process, using the flow chart in the Student Book to guide you. Ask the class to help you to decide: which of the quotations is the most relevant in supporting the point being made? Pairs of students should continue to select the most relevant quotation to support the points detailed in the Student Book, using points 1–5 of the flow chart to guide them. After each statement, the pair should try to decide which of the relevant quotations is the most relevant.

Introduction (15 minutes)

Turn to page 115 of the Student Book: the pen portraits of two Superheroes. In pairs, students read the texts aloud, swapping after each sentence. Explain to the students that you are going to make this next section of the lesson more challenging: in the last activity the statements about the text were given to the students. This time, the students will have to make the statements themselves **and** find relevant evidence to support their comments.

Model aloud the process of making a response to the first question about the portraits, discarding non-relevant information and identifying some relevant quotations, before selecting the **most** relevant quotation to support your comment. In pairs, students should take it in turns to answer a question and, speaking their thoughts aloud as they have been shown, scan the texts for relevant evidence, before selecting the most relevant quotation. Their partner should listen to them and watch what they do, using the flow chart from the first session of the lesson to offer guidance if their partner becomes lost or gets 'stuck'. They should swap roles after each question.

Development (20 minutes)

Recap: so, as the students know, one of the ways they can back up their ideas or comments about a text is by using relevant quotations. But as they also know, sometimes quotations are not appropriate because a big section of the text is relevant and the quotation would be too long. In these cases they can use paraphrase; they can retell a part of the text to back up a point.

Turn to page 116 of the Student Book. Read the article as a class and use the example question and paraphrase to model the process of answering the question and backing up your answer without making a direct quotation. Make it clear that you have chosen to paraphrase because there is too big a chunk of relevant information to put in a direct quotation. Give each student a copy of the questions (resource sheet 1.1). Allow them two minutes to read the questions, underlining the most important words. They need to consider what their answers might be and which part of the text they might go to for their answers. Pair the students up to talk about their answers to the questions and to point out where in the text they would look for their evidence. Next, allow students to leave their seats to ask one another the questions. In answer to a question, they must make a response and back it up by paraphrasing details in the text, using the prompts on the question sheets to help them.

Lesson Plan 1 of 3

To know how to identify and comment on writers' purposes and use of language

Secure competent reader

Cycle D

Duration: 1 hour

Plenary (10 minutes)

End the lesson by returning to the second paragraph of the article and the 'Ask yourself' questions on page 117 of the Student Book. Give the students one minute to remind themselves: When should we use a quotation? When should we use a paraphrase? Share responses and clarify. Individually, students should read the 'Ask yourself' questions, identify the key word in each, look at the second paragraph and try to decide whether the response to the question should be backed up by paraphrase or quotation. After three minutes, pair the students up and allow them to share their decisions. Can they justify them? Do they agree? Clarify any disagreement as a class.

Lesson Plan
2 of 3

To know how to identify and comment on writers' purposes and use of language: to be able to paraphrase

Secure competent reader

Cycle D

Duration: 1 hour

Resources needed	Lesson aims	Assessment Focuses
• CD-ROM Cycle D (Secure competent reader) resource sheet 2.1: cut-up cards, one set per pair of students • Student Book pages 118–119: 'What's your opinion?' • CD-ROM Cycle D (Secure competent reader) resource sheet 2.2: 'Is this film worth seeing?' diagram and prompt questions	• to be able to make some comments about the effects and purposes of a writer's choice of language **Target areas** • Target area 3: Identifying and commenting on a writer's choice of language	AF5

Starter (15 minutes)

Explain to the students that today they are going to investigate how the words a writer chooses can show us how the writer feels about something or someone. Give the students one minute's thinking time in response to the question: 'How much do you like ice-cream?' Hand out the cut-up cards from resource sheet 2.1 to pairs of students. Explain to the students that 12 very different people were asked whether they liked ice-cream: these words are taken from their responses. In pairs, students should read the words and see if they can place them in order from 10/10 I **love** ice-cream, to 0/10 I **hate** ice-cream. Model aloud the thought process involved in taking the first word and placing it on the spectrum from 1 to 10. Point out that the students might have to change the order of their words as they work through the activity. The only rule is that if they place a word or change the place of a word, they must explain their thinking. Join pairs to form groups of four, taking with them their continuum of words. Pairs compare their decisions: where are the major differences? Can they persuade the other pair that their order is more fitting? Do they need to change their order? Recap by reinforcing the idea that the language that we choose can communicate how we feel about something, whether we feel positively about it, negatively or whether we aren't really bothered.

Introduction (15 minutes)

Write the following clearly on the board: *This pizza tastes disgusting. I'll give it 10/10.* Give the students 30 seconds' individually to consider the question: What is the problem with this opinion?' Allow the students to pair and share briefly, before modelling the process of a) identifying the problem by underlining the problem items b) explaining the problem as clearly as possible and c) putting the problem right, by changing the mark out of 10 to reflect the word 'disgusting'. Make sure that you model all thought processes aloud. Ask the class if they can think of other ways to solve the problem (e.g. by changing the word to match the 10/10 score) and take suggestions for a word that could replace *disgusting*.

Turn to page 118 of the Student Book. Organise the students into groups of three. They should take it in turns to play the three different roles 1, 2 and 3 in the flow chart, working through the opinions in the Student Book. They must speak their thoughts aloud, so that their team-mates can understand where their decisions have come from. Ask the students what they have learnt from doing this activity: record their thinking on the board. Next, give individual students two minutes to choose a topic that they have an opinion on: a TV programme, a band, a fashion item. They need to come up with a star rating for the thing they are giving their opinion on and a statement that fits the star rating. They can use the examples in the Student Book, if they find it difficult to shape their ideas. Above all, they must think carefully about their choice of words. Allow the students to move from their chairs and swap opinions and star ratings with others: do they agree that the star ratings and the language of the opinion 'fit'? If they hear something they don't agree with, they must challenge it politely, explain their thinking and a suggest a way to fix the problem.

Development (20 minutes)

Turn the students' attention to the film review in the Student Book. Explain a little of how film reviews come to be written, the kinds of places they are published, who they are written by and why they are written. Point out that this film review does not yet have a rating (a mark out of 10 reflecting

To know how to identify and comment on writers' purposes and use of language: to be able to paraphrase

Secure competent reader

Cycle D

Duration: 1 hour

what the reviewer thought of the film). Did this reviewer think that the film was worth 10/10? 5/10? 1/10? Hand out resource sheet 2.2, one per student. Model aloud the thought processes involved in reading the first paragraph of the review, sentence by sentence, identifying words that might give an indication of the reviewer's opinion of the film. Show how these words should be recorded on the handout. Individually, students should continue reading the review, sentence by sentence, identifying and recording words that give an indication of how the reviewer felt about the film. After ten minutes, re-call the attention of the class and ask: 'Based on the words you have picked out, what rating out of 10 should this film get?' Explain to the students that they have to find a best fit number out of 10. Give them one minute to think before asking them to decide. Using the prompts at the bottom of the handout, students should practise explaining the rating they have given to the film based on the language of the review and explain how they came to that decision: their explanation needs to be fluent enough for an audience to hear it. Turn the students' attention to the 'Ask yourself' box in the Student Book. Pair the students up so that they can share their decisions and the reasons behind it.

Plenary (10 minutes)

Finally, students should spend five minutes individually recording their response in writing using full sentences; they can use the prompts provided to help them. After five minutes' writing, they should swap with a partner: the 'Ask yourself' box should be used to give feedback on what has been done well.

Lesson Plan 3 of 3

To know how to identify and comment on writers' purposes and use of language

Secure competent reader

Cycle D

Duration: 1 hour

Resources needed	Lesson aims	Assessment Focuses
• Student Book pages 120–121: 'Using your research skills' • CD-ROM Cycle D (Secure competent reader) resource sheet 3.1: research organiser, one per student	• to know how to carry out research using several sources • to understand how to paraphrase or retell, to support comment • to be able to understand a writer's viewpoint **Target areas** • Target area 4: Understanding a writer's viewpoint	AF2, AF5

Starter (15 minutes)

Explain to the students that in this lesson they are going to be practising a number of the new reading skills they have learnt over the past few weeks: they will be undertaking some independent research using three different texts, they will be using paraphrase to support their comments about those texts and they will be focusing on the different writers' viewpoints. Turn to page 120 of the Student Book and set up the lesson's scenario: the students are sports journalists working for a radio show; their job is to prepare reports on local events to be read during the news bulletins each hour. Give individual students one minute to think: what should we do **before** we begin any research? Pair and share and feedback ideas to the board. If the students do not mention the need to be really clear about what they are researching, point this out and explain the reasons behind it. As a class, read the email from the editor on page 120 of the Student Book. In pairs, students should come up with a list of questions about the cricket match they will want to find the answers for by researching. Share as a class and make a list on the board: model aloud the thought processes involved in deciding on the top three most important questions, in your opinion (explain to the students that they will need to make their own choices). Hand out copies of the research organiser on resource sheet 3.1. Give the students two minutes to discuss in pairs whether they think this organiser will be useful to them in researching what happened at this match: which parts of the organiser might be useful? Can they make any suggestions about how to improve it? Feedback ideas to the board and then allow the students to tailor the organiser, if they wish.

Introduction (15 minutes)

Ask the students what they remember about 'the writer's point of view'. Give individuals 30 seconds to think before sharing with a partner to clarify and then feedback their clarified ideas to the board. Pair up the students and allow them to read through the three texts. Turn the students' attention to the questions about the different writers' opinions of the cricket match on page 121 of the Student Book. Taking the first question as an example, use the flow chart to model the thought processes involved in answering one of these questions, using paraphrase to support the answer you give. Allow individual students five minutes to tackle the remaining questions, using the flow chart to guide them. Take feedback to the whole class, clarifying the idea of different writers having different viewpoints as often as possible by saying: 'Yes, this writer has a different view of the match … this writer feels very differently about how the home team played …This writer's viewpoint is different.' Next, return the students' attention to their research organiser: they need to choose and record their three key research questions in the table. Allow the students eight minutes to undertake their research, working independently.

Development (20 minutes)

The students now need to write their match report, as the deadline of the first evening news bulletin is fast approaching. They will need to give an overview of the match and use paraphrase to back up their comments. Model the process of deciding how you will report the match (It went well? It went badly?) and write the first line of the report, explaining which details you are paraphrasing. Using the stems in the 'Assess your progress' box on page 121 of the Student Book to help them, students should draft their own report.

Lesson Plan 3 of 3

To know how to identify and comment on writers' purposes and use of language

Secure competent reader

Cycle D

Duration: 1 hour

Plenary (10 minutes)
Ask one of the more confident members of the class to share their news report (perhaps you could write it up on the board?) and model the process of identifying where the student has paraphrased information from one of the statements. Working with a partner, the students should share their reports and then help one another to identify the examples of paraphrase that have been used, tracing them back to details in the original statements.

Consolidation and assessment

Lesson Plan 1 of 3

Secure competent reader

Assessment

Duration: 1 hour

Resources needed	Lesson aims	Framework Objectives
• Teacher's Guide page 145: cut-up cards • Student Book pages 122–123: 'Have my reading skills improved?' • Teacher's Guide page 146: OHT • Teacher's Guide page 147: text for students to annotate, one per student	• to be able to independently select reading skills to make meaning **Target areas** • Target area 1: Inference and deduction • Target area 2: Using textual evidence to support inference	**Assessment Focuses** AF2, AF3

Starter (15 minutes)

Turn to page 122 of the Student Book and use the metaphor of the backpack to enable the students to perceive themselves as readers with a range of skills at their fingertips. Use the success criteria in the backpack image to remind them of some of the reading skills they have learnt and developed during the past few weeks and should therefore be carrying around with them in their backpack. Organise the students into pairs and give a set of cards from page 145 of the Teacher's Guide to each pair. Give students five minutes to use the 'Ask yourself' questions on page 122 of the Student Book to sort their cards and to discuss their responses. Draw together the responses to the final two questions: **Why** are these skills important? **When** might we use these reading skills? Explain to the students that over the course of the next three lessons they will need to become increasingly independent in the way they use their reading skills.

Introduction (15 minutes)

Explain to the students that during the next three lessons they will read and respond to a story, the opening section of which is printed on page 123 of the Student Book. Give individual students one minute to think before pairing and sharing: 'What does a reader want to know at the beginning of a story?' Feedback the key point from each pair to the board. Working in a different pair, allow the students two minutes to discuss which reading skills they could use to find this information. Feedback some of their thinking to the board, making sure you emphasise the importance of making decisions about **how** to read, selecting from the backpack of skills they carry with them as readers. Displaying the first two paragraphs of the story (found on page 146 of the Teacher's guide) on a projector, read the first two sentences aloud to the class and model aloud the thought processes involved in choosing and using reading strategies to make sense of these sentences by saying, 'I will use ... because ...'. Pairs of students should continue this process, taking a sentence at a time and selecting a reading skill from their 'backpack' to apply to the sentence. Allow pairs to join up into groups of four to share what they have discovered from the first paragraph of the story and to explain **how** they reached this understanding of the meaning.

Development (20 minutes)

Turn the students' attention to the second section of the story on page 123 of the Student Book, where they will find the next two paragraphs of the story. Hand out a copy of page 147 of the Teacher's Guide, one per student, for annotation. Use the example already done on the resource as an example of how the students need to work. Students should read and annotate for ten minutes before pairing up with another student to share their insights about the story. At the end of this session, use the 'what's the story' question to draw the class' understanding together. Ask the class 'which of these questions requires a literal reading of the text? Which require a non-literal reading?'

Plenary (10 minutes)

Explain to the students that, as a class, they are going to use their ideas about what is happening in the story to speculate and predict what might happen next. Begin by asking one of the students to share a reading/discovery they have made about the story so far, encouraging the students to build on each

Assessment

Duration: 1 hour

other's ideas or gently disagree if they have different ideas. Turn next to the process of making a prediction based on one of these ideas, allowing one student to start the process off again, before the others chip in, building on or challenging. Return to the success criteria: which of these skills have the students used this lesson? Which of the skills did they struggle with? Encourage the students to set an individual target for next lesson.

Cut-up cards: reading skills

	I can visualise the text, 'seeing' the ideas in my mind.	I can support the comments I make about a text by paraphrasing or retelling a part of the text.
I can make links between the text and my own experiences.	I can place myself in the shoes of characters and feel what they are feeling.	I can ask questions of a text to help me dig beneath the surface meaning.
I can make inferences, reading *beneath the surface* of the text.	I can support the comments I make about a text with a quotation.	I can make deductions about a text by making links between the details in a text.

Secure competent reader

'Don't be a hero': opening paragraph for display

Her mum, gran and younger brother had disappeared in their beaten-up saloon car into the muddle of twisting Cornish lanes just after breakfast. They were on a trip to Padstow.

'And don't be heroes,' her gran's gravel voice had said from deep inside the car. 'The world has enough dead heroes. You look out for yourselves, hear?' And they'd driven off, due to return around tea-time. A surprising period of freedom stretched ahead. Amy had no idea what to do with it.

Secure competent reader

'Don't be a hero': text for students to annotate

a Which reading skills am I using at each point of the story?

I am reading beneath the surface.

Luke was supposed to look after Amy. He was older, stronger. But that holiday he had been strangely jumpy and nervous, especially when Sian was around. Sian and her family were staying two caravans along in a 'deluxe 1200' with a flat-screen TV and flushing toilet. Luke's eyes were always searching Sian out.

b What do I understand about this story?

I think that Luke has been left in charge: his mum has given him responsibility.

So that day it was no real surprise when Amy found herself trailing behind her brother down to the beach to 'accidentally' bump into Sian. Around her stood a group of the friends she had made since she arrived five days earlier. They were trying to organise a party that evening, arguing about where to hold it. No one noticed Luke's arrival. Amy stood a little way off and watched her brother's strange shyness. After five minutes of being ignored, he tried to get the group's attention.

Consolidation and assessment

Secure competent reader

Assessment

Duration: 1 hour

Resources needed	Lesson aims	Assessment Focuses
• Teacher's Guide page 150: cut-up cards, one set per pair of students • Teacher's Guide page 151: OHT • Student Book pages 122–125: 'Have my reading skills improved?' • Teacher's Guide page 152: one copy per student	• to be able to independently select reading skills in order to decipher meaning **Target areas** • Target area 1: Inference and deduction • Target area 2: Using textual evidence to support inference • Target area 3: Identifying and commenting on a writer's choice of language	AF2, AF3, AF5

Starter (15 minutes)

Turn to page 124 of the Student Book and remind the students of the backpack, encouraging them to perceive themselves as readers with a range of skills at their fingertips. Explain that in this lesson, they will focus on using more of the reading skills that they have learnt in the past few weeks and should therefore be carrying around with them in their backpack. Organise the students into pairs and give each pair a set of cards from page 150 of the Teacher's Guide. Give them five minutes to use the 'Ask yourself' questions on page 122 of the Student Book to sort their cards and discuss their responses. Draw together the responses to the final two questions: '**Why** are these skills important? **When** might we use these reading skills?' Explain to the students that over the course of the next two lessons they will need to become increasingly independent in the way they use their reading skills.

Introduction (15 minutes)

Allow individual students two minutes to remind themselves of the story so far, using the prompt questions on page 123 of the Student Book. Displaying page 151 of the Teacher's Guide on a projector, model aloud the thought processes involved in answering the question: 'What is Luke feeling when he tells the others about the sea-caves?' Explain to the students that there might be more than one answer to this question: you will have to investigate the text in detail. Follow the flow chart to guide your responses and ensure that the students understand that you are using it, annotating the text with notes about your responses as you go. After five minutes of reading/responding to/annotating the text, allow pairs of students to talk through your findings: which of the 'answers' to the question do they feel is most important? Explain to the students that you are going to model the process of turning one of the answers into a paragraph explaining that idea in detail. Use the PEE response on the right-hand side of page 151 of the Teacher's Guide to model, uncovering one stage of the PEE process at a time. Ask the students to use the success criteria in the backpack image on page 124 of the Student Book to judge the response on the projected page: which skills have been successfully used?

Development (20 minutes)

Turn the students' attention to the next section of the story on page 125 of the Student Book. Explain to the students that they are going to have a go at independently responding to this section of the story, as you have modelled for them. Hand out copies of the next section of the story from page 152 of the Teacher's Guide, one per student. Allow individual students eight minutes to read, use their skills and make notes. Organise the students into pairs and allow them to build their confidence by explaining to a partner the answers that they have found. Next, using the PEE guidance and the stems on page 127 of the Student Book, individual students should have a go at turning one of their points into a written paragraph.

Plenary (10 minutes)

Return to the 'backpack' of successful reading skills in the Student Book, from both this lesson and the previous one. Pair the students up so that they can share their written responses to the question: 'Which of the success criteria have they been successful in meeting?' Which do they still need to work

Consolidation and assessment

Secure competent reader

Assessment

Duration: 1 hour

on? Their written responses should be collected in so that their understanding can be formally assessed by the teacher. Use the assessments to set targets for the students.

Secure competent reader

Cut-up cards for pairs of students

I can make predictions about a text, based on my ideas.	I can understand a writer's point of view.	I can make comments about the words that a writer specially chooses.
I can wonder/speculate about the ideas in texts.	I can identify some of the words that a writer specially chooses.	

Secure competent reader

What is Luke feeling when he tells the others about the sea-caves?

1 Read the question

2 Read a sentence or two from the text

3 Choose a reading skill from your backpack that will help you

4 Jot down your ideas in response to the text

'There are sea-caves, you know.' The first time he said it, Luke wasn't heard. Their voices rattled on around him as though he was just another pebble on the beach. Only Amy saw his hunched shoulders and noticed his darting eyes. He tried again: 'Have you heard about the caves?' The tallest boy, with blond hair the colour of sand, turned to face Luke, whose gaze fell immediately. The boy had a look of boredom on his long freckled face.

'So, what are you saying?' demanded the tall boy in a voice that sounded tight. Amy saw her brother's eyes flick to Sian's face and back again to meet the blond boy's gaze.

'Well, my family has been here before – to this holiday beach, I mean ... and ... and there are sea caves that lead through to another beach that would be really good for a party. I know the way through the caves.' As Luke spoke, his words ran fast, out of control.

'Sea caves. I like that idea.' Sian's voice was picked up and blown by the wind so that Amy could hear the syrup sweetness of her voice.

'Are you sure you know these caves?' The tall boy's arms were folded across his chest and his eyes were hard.

'It might take me a while to remember – but I do know them.' Luke replied quickly.

'Ha! He doesn't know.' The tall boy's laughter set some of the others off grinning.

'I do. I do know them. I do,' Luke begged.

'We'll see, won't we? We'll be outside the shop at six.' Following their leader, the group turned away and clambered up over the sand bank. Their arms were interlocked and their hands rested on each others' shoulders.

Point:
Luke feels nervou
when he tells the
group about the s
caves.

Evidence:
I can tell this whe
says in the text, '
Amy saw his hun
shoulders and his
darting eyes.'

Explain:
The word 'darting
reminds me of th
movement of a
frightened fish. I
that the writer w
to show that Luk
nervous about go
into the caves. B
is also nervous a
being left out of
group. I predict t
Luke will go to th
caves, even thou
is scared, becaus
is more scared of
others thinking th
is weak.

Secure competent reader

How does Amy feel as Luke walks away from her towards the sea-caves?

1 Read the question

2 Read a sentence or two from the text

3 Choose a reading skill from your backpack that will help you

4 Jot down your ideas in response to the text

Amy watched the group disappear over the sand dune, their voices fading so that only the sound of the waves reached her ears. She turned to an empty space on the sand, her brother already marching away towards the water. She called after him.

'I'm going.' This was all Luke said, his jaw tight.

'But, Mum said – ' The promises that she and Luke had made just an hour ago were nagging at Amy's mind.

'I'm going.'

'But, Luke – remember last year. Remember the helicopter and everything. It was on the news. Those people were lucky to escape with their lives, the coastguard said. Remember? Luke!' By now he had reached the mouth of the passage between the cliff and the island. Amy allowed her cupped hands to drop from her mouth and slapped her arms hard against her sides.

'I'm going!' Luke's voice was as hard as the blond boy's had been.

'But, Luke,' Amy's words rasped in her throat as she threw them across the sand, 'THE TIDE!' The water was already creeping over the sand, inch by inch with each new wave. It looked like a calm and soft blanket when you viewed the open sands of the whole bay like this. But in the gully between the steep cliffs and the sides of the island, Amy knew the water would surge and froth, sucking away from the rocks like lips drawing back over jagged teeth.

Amy watched Luke's tanned back as he clambered around the rough edges of the first rock pools. The bones of his spine stretched the skin as he reached down to balance himself over a tricky gully. He is so young, Amy thought. She called to him a final time, her fists clenched at her sides, but he showed no sign of hearing her.

Lesson Plan
3 of 3

Consolidation and assessment

Secure competent reader

Assessment

Duration: 1 hour

Resources needed	Lesson aims	Assessment Focuses
• Student Book pages 126–127: 'Is my reading improving?' • Teacher's Guide page 154: OHT • Teacher's Guide page 155: one copy per student	• to be able to independently comment on the writer's use of language • to understand the writer's viewpoint **Target areas** • Target area 3: Identifying and commenting on a writer's choice of language • Target area 4: Understanding a writer's viewpoint	AF2, AF3, AF5, AF6

Starter (15 minutes)

Show the students the image of the backpack on page 124 of the Student Book. Give individuals one minute to think about the question: 'What do we mean by the reader's backpack of skills?' Pair and share before feeding back the key ideas to the class to clarify. Draw attention to the 'Assess your progress' box on page 127 of the Student Book: explain that these are the skills the students will need to use in this lesson. Allow pairs of students five minutes to remember the story so far, using the questions on page 126 of the Student Book to prompt their recap. As a class, discuss the possible directions the story could now go in: map the ideas on the board, using arrows to show the direction of ideas and double lines to show the links between ideas. Read the next part of the story, on page 126 of the Student Book. What happens next? Are any of the students' predictions correct so far?

Introduction (15 minutes)

Display page 154 of the Teacher's Guide on a projector; model aloud the thought processes involved in answering the question: 'How does the writer show us that the caves are a dangerous place to be?' Model the annotation of the text with your ideas about the words chosen by the writer to create a sense of danger, using the flow chart at the top of the resource to guide you. After five minutes of reading/responding to/annotating the text, allow pairs of students to talk through your findings: which of the writer's words do they feel is most important in creating a sense of danger? Explain to the students that you are going to model the process of turning one of the answers into a paragraph explaining that idea in detail. Use the PEE response on the right hand side pf the OHT to model, uncovering one stage of the PEE process at a time. Ask students to return to the 'Assess your progress' box in the Student Book to judge the response on the projected page: which skills have been successfully used?

Development (20 minutes)

Turn the students' attention to the next paragraph of the story on page 127 of the Student Book. Explain to the students that they are going to have a go at independently responding to this section of the story, as you have modelled for them. Give each student a copy of the next section of the story from page 155 of the Teacher's Guide. Allow individual students eight minutes to read, use their skills and make notes. Pair the students up and allow them to build their confidence by explaining to a partner the answers that they have found. Next, using the PEE guidance and the stems in the Student Book, individual students should have a go at turning one of their points into a written paragraph.

Plenary (10 minutes)

Return to the reading success criteria in the backpack image in the Student Book. Pair the students up so that they can share their written responses to the question: 'Which of the success criteria have they been successful in meeting? Which do they still need to work on?' The students' written responses should then be collected in so that their understanding can be formally assessed by the teacher.

Secure competent reader

How does the writer show us that the caves are a dangerous place to be? (1)

1. Read the question carefully, underlining the key words
2. Read a sentence of the text
3. Identify words carefully chosen by the writer that fit with the question
4. Think about what the key word suggests, why the writer has used it
5. Make notes on your ideas

After an hour, Luke had not returned and Amy made her way reluctantly down the slope of sand towards the gully. The incoming tide was already ankle deep at this point. On the left towered the cliffs and on the right lay the jagged banks of the island. Up ahead giant fireworks of white froth exploded against the walls. The waves rolled in one after another from the open sea. From the sheltered beach the water always seemed friendly and tame. Here the sea was a beast. White gulls, nesting on the cliffs above wheeled angrily just a few metres over Amy's head. Everything about this place said, 'DO NOT PASS!'

Point:
The gully that Amy enters seems dangerous.

Evidence:
The writer has used the word 'narrow' to describe the gully.

Explain:
This word makes me think that Amy or Luke might become stuck or trapped in the gully, and I worry about their safety. In my mind I see the sides of the gully like a tunnel. 'Narrow' makes the gully seem risky. I think that this word shows that Amy is feeling closed in and panicked.

Secure competent reader

How does the writer show us that the caves are a dangerous place to be? (2)

1 Read the question carefully, underlining the key words

2 Read a sentence of the text

3 Identify words carefully chosen by the writer that fit with the question

4 Think about what the key word suggests, why the writer has used it

5 Make notes on your ideas

Amy reached the darkened opening of the cave after a few minutes. It looked smaller than she remembered. She inched along a ledge of rock before squatting at the ragged entrance, her hand resting on the cold, flat surface of the wet rock.

'Lu-uke!' Her voice echoed just as she remembered, sounding hollow and odd. Amy slithered down the tumble of rocks and into the darkness. She used her toes to grip but this meant that she cut the base of her feet on the sharp barnacle shells which covered every surface. The waves pulled at her feet on the slippery rocks, spitting salt high into the air. Her anger blazed. Why was she playing the hero? She should have called the lifeguards instead of trying to play the champion. She thought of Sian, of her styled hair, her fashionable clothes and her winning smile. Was it Sian's fault that Luke was alone somewhere in the caves and that Amy was crouched here with bleeding feet, the water rising with every minute that passed?

'Lu-u-uke!' There was no answer: only the deep boom of the waves crashing against the cliff face.

